"I am fascinated by what Timothy O'Malley has done in this book, espousing Luigi Giussani's visionary insights to the RCIA process. How can the Christian initiation process provoke a deeper desire for God? How can the catechumenate propose a more human life anchored in Christ? How can catechumens verify the truth of this proposal so that they might respond by making a gift of their lives? O'Malley argues persuasively that not only is the RCIA inclined towards these questions, the liturgy itself forms us along this trajectory. This book is a must read for all those invested in the RCIA, but also for each of us who desires to truly live the Christian life."

—Dr. James Pauley
    Professor of Theology and Catechetics
    Franciscan University of Steubenville

Divine Blessing

Liturgical Formation in the RCIA

Timothy P. O'Malley

LITURGICAL PRESS
Collegeville, Minnesota

www.litpress.org

Library of Congress Cataloging-in-Publication Data

Names: O'Malley, Timothy P., author.
Title: Divine blessing : liturgical formation in the RCIA / Timothy P. O'Malley.
Description: Collegeville : Liturgical Press, 2019. | Includes bibliographical references.
Identifiers: LCCN 2018042877 | ISBN 9780814663615 (pbk.)
Subjects: LCSH: Catholic Church. Ordo initiationis Christianae adultorum. | Initiation rites—Religious aspects—Catholic Church.
Classification: LCC BX2045.I553 O43 2019 | DDC 264/.020813—dc23
LC record available at https://lccn.loc.gov/2018042877

For Maxwell Johnson—mentor, scholar, minister, and friend

Contents

Introduction

During graduate work, I took an intensive summer course in the ancient liturgical language Syriac. Like Hebrew, Syriac is read from right to left. In the early days of the course, it took effort to retrain my eyes to read in this way. Successfully deciphering Syriac was not reducible to memorizing grammatical rules. It was a physical undertaking whereby I developed a new habit of moving my eyes over a page from right to left. Learning to read in this way took hour after hour of practicing the exhausting craft.

Learning this new way of reading had global effects. I began deciphering each English word as if it were written in Syriac from right to left. A STOP sign became POTS. My spouse's name, Kara, became A-RAK. The church on Notre Dame's campus was the ACI-LI-SAB. As my spouse can attest, I was an annoying passenger to schlep around town.

Formation in the *Rite of Christian Initiation of Adults* involves a similar comprehensive retraining of the way we perceive the world. We don't just read texts. We read everything. We make judgments each day, both small and large, about the meaning of life's happenings. Dark clouds rolling in on a beautiful spring day portend thunderstorms. A stop sign on a road declares to us that our vehicle must come to a complete and absolute stop for the safety of cars, other pedestrians, and ourselves. A crucifix around someone's neck reveals that he or she might be Christian.

To be human is to be a reader of such signs. But as readers of signs, we know that we can make mistakes. Sometimes, we don't yet understand the meaning of a particular sign. If I hold my hand out to vigorously shake the hand of an infant, I should not be aghast if the infant responds with a blank stare. We travel to a foreign country, trying to decipher the word for "bathroom" and "restaurant" lest we confuse the two. To a novice, the game of soccer is nothing but rarely kicking a ball into a goal; but to the soccer aficionado, the beautiful game involves thousands of smaller competitions and strategies that delight and entertain. All of education, entrance into a culture, involves learning to read signs.

But this education is not reducible to the act of mental gymnastics. As readers of signs, our whole self is often involved. Imagine someone who has an addiction to shopping for shoes. His or her closet is full of black, brown, gray, green, blue, and orange tennis shoes, boots, flats, heels, and sandals. This person *loves* shoes. *Hopes* for more shoes. *Desires* shoes. In fact, the desire is so strong that each time this person goes to the mall, the only objects that occupy the attention of our footgear devotee are the shoed feet of passersby and the rich smell of leather coming from shoe stores.

Learning to read signs involves an education into a certain way of desiring. Our servant to the gods of footwear may experience a conversion one day, recognizing that such exclusive focus on boots, flats, and heels has led not to increased happiness but to a diminished bank account. The former shoe-lover would need to discover a new way of "reading" the meaning of footwear— shoes are used fundamentally for walking and only secondarily for adornment. This reeducation will not be immediate. It will require learning to desire something else—whether that be a less full closet, a fuller bank account, or a simpler way of life.

The RCIA provides this reformation of desire, this education of learning to read signs well, through the church's liturgy. Formation in the Christian life is an often painful process of discovering what is worth loving in the first place. We Christians are a funny sort that adore not at the altar of political power or the throne of economic efficiency. We worship the God who reveals the power of powerlessness in God's birth as infant, in dying as a human being, in being raised up from the dead through the power of the Spirit. We give praise to the God who operates according to, not a scarce economy, but a gratuitous economy of gift. It shouldn't surprise us that learning to adore this God of self-giving love might take a process of reeducation.

Liturgical formation is integral to the RCIA because it's at the heart of Christian life. St. Paul in his letter to the Romans exhorts Christians "to offer your bodies as a living sacrifice, holy and pleasing to God, your spiritual worship. Do not conform yourselves to this age but be transformed by the renewal of your mind, that you may discern what is the will of God, what is good and pleasing and perfect" (Rom 12:1-2). The Christian is to see the entire world as a sign pointing toward the reality of God's love. Creation is a place of gift, of meaning, of hope, and of love. The proper response to this love is to offer the entire self in return. The gift of our entire self is the one gift that God really wants.

Learning the grammar of the worshipful orientation of Christian life requires basic knowledge of the signs. But it also necessitates a deeper formation. We are meant to become a "living sacrifice" to God. That's the ultimate end of the RCIA because it's the very meaning of Christian life! We human beings are made for self-giving love.

Liturgy as Curriculum

It is easy to forget, based on present pastoral practice, that the RCIA is concerned about the formation of human beings into a new way of life grounded in Christ. Too often our approach to the RCIA suffers from one of two temptations. First, we focus on a single task of catechesis: knowledge of the faith. We teach people how to decipher the signs. Catechumens and candidates for full communion are given a short course in Christian doctrine, the sacraments, the moral life, and practices of prayer. This education is conducted in a classroom where ideas are presented but never lived out. The sign is understood, while the desire of the catechumen remains unaffected.

A second temptation exists around the language of experience. In The Joy of the Gospel, Pope Francis notes that the "primary reason for evangelizing is the love of Jesus which we have received, the experience of salvation which urges us to ever greater love of him" (EG 264). The encounter with Jesus Christ in the church is meant to take up every dimension of our being—our feelings, our intellect, and our will. Conversion to Christ is a powerful experience in which we discover the presence of the risen Lord, changing the way we engage in everything. But there is a temptation to understand the "powerful experience" as the locus of the encounter. Not every aspect of the Christian life will be full of feeling. There are dry spells in our prayer. There is the mundane task of going to Mass on Sunday, of feeding and caring for poor persons, and of living together in the community of the parish.

The initiatory catechesis of the RCIA must include a systematic account of what constitutes Christian life that avoids both dry didacticism and an excessive emphasis on individual feelings. As *The General Directory for Catechesis* (GDC) describes:

> This comprehensive formation includes more than instruction: it is an apprenticeship of the entire Christian life, it is a "complete Christian initiation," which promotes an authentic following of Christ, focused on his Person; it implies education in knowledge of the faith and in the life of faith, in such a manner that the entire person, at his deepest levels, feels enriched by the word of God; it helps the disciple of Christ to transform the old man in order to assume his baptismal responsibilities and to profess the faith from the "heart." (68)

Formation in the RCIA is conversion, training the disciple to take on a new form of life in Christ. Its final end is profession of faith with the fullness of heart. This means our whole being including our bodies, our minds, our affections, and our wills given over to God.

Liturgical formation is essential to this apprenticeship in the Christian life. In the liturgy, we encounter the doctrines of the church through embodied practice. Christmas manifests to us the incarnation of Jesus Christ. On Good Friday, we learn what it means to say that God has died. And on Easter, we understand the resurrection of the Word made flesh through Alleluias that ring out all over the world. We are also asked to reconsider what constitutes human happiness as we celebrate the mystery of Christ's death and resurrection in the liturgical year. Liturgical prayer is something that we're supposed to think about. What does it mean for me that the Word became flesh at Christmas? What can I learn about sacrifice through Easter? We discover new ways of living our day-to-day lives through practices of worship that spill over into the home. A Christian is not someone who expresses abstract confidence in theoretical systems of belief. A Christian perceives, thinks, and acts as a Christian in the world.

The church's liturgy, therefore, is not just one of the things that needs to be taught in the RCIA. By means of careful liturgical formation throughout the process, the catechumens or candidates receive the fullness of a Christian personality. They become the kind of persons who can read the "signs" of the world aright. As Catholic philosopher and theologian Dietrich von Hildebrand remarks, "The conscious, fully awakened act of performing the Liturgy imprints upon the soul the Face of Christ. In taking part in the Liturgy, we make our own the fundamental attitudes embodied in it" (*Liturgy and Personality*, 11). Liturgy is the school of discipleship in which we find ourselves practicing the embodied art of self-giving love through kneeling, marking our body with the sign of the cross, and giving our voices over to the praise and adoration of the living God.

Liturgy's Pedagogy: Provocation, Hypothesis, and Verification

How does liturgy teach? How does the act of praying together in the liturgy work toward a mature Christian faith? One way of answering these questions is to rely on the educational insights of Fr. Luigi Giussani (1922–2005), the founder of the Catholic movement Communion and Liberation. A priest, professor, spiritual director, high school teacher, and mentor to thousands, Giussani developed an approach to Christian education that is fully human, grounded in the story of salvation revealed in Jesus Christ, and appropriated through learning to live in friendship in the church (Savorana, *The Life of Luigi Giussani*).

Although Giussani did not write extensively on the liturgy, he did place baptism at the center of his understanding of Christian education. He recognized that baptism reoriented the Christian toward a new reality. He writes:

> Nothing is more radically decisive for human existence than this fact called Baptism—a fact so real that its external effect can be wholly described: it has a precise date; it physically took hold of us in a given moment. Like any fact, it may appear to be something very fragile. . . . But with that Event called Baptism, something irreducibly new began in us. It is a real Event that enters a situation and changes it, then determines it in a new way. (Giussani, Alberto, and Prades, *Generating Traces in the History of the World*, 46–47)

Initiation into the church brings about a new way of seeing the world. Have you ever stopped for a moment and thought to yourself, "I really exist"? The things that happen to us each day are real, not only figments of overactive imaginations. The actions we perform have consequences, not in some universe far away, but in our day-to-day world. For the Christian, baptism should awaken us to an even deeper reality than the existence of the world. As St. Paul attests, "no longer I, but Christ lives in me; insofar as I now live in the flesh, I live by faith in the Son of God who has loved me and given himself up for me" (Gal 2:20). Formation for baptism should prepare the Christian to live not as an isolated "I" but as someone whose whole life has been taken up with Christ. My daily decisions, every thought, every action is to manifest divine love.

Christian formation, for Giussani, thus cannot be separated from human formation. We must think through how our "I" has been transformed by the encounter with Christ's "Thou." Giussani argues that every act of good education begins with provocation. Provocation doesn't mean trying to get a rise out of someone—it would be an unwise provocative to yell "Let's Go Sox" in the middle of Yankee Stadium. A proper sense of provocation requires taking the risk of looking at reality for what it is. Anyone who has held a newborn child can recognize the way that this experience provokes us toward the deepest questions: What really matters now that this child exists in my life? How will I live after this encounter? Every human being is born with this natural religious sense. And the educational task of provocation brings us face-to-face with the "really real," with the questions that matter. Provocation is the first step of seeing the world even in all its messiness for what it is—a gift to be contemplated (Giussani, *The Religious Sense*, 101).

For Giussani, such questions are not the ultimate end of Christian formation. After all, questions may not merely reveal. They may hide too. A certain critical attitude can arise in which we question whether anything exists beyond scientific reason. The question "But how do I know that she loves me?" often functions in this manner. The Christian educator does not succumb to this temptation. Instead, the catechist dares to suggest that there is something about the Christian story that provides an answer to life's deepest questions. The educator offers a hypothesis. Giussani writes, "Only an educational approach that introduces human and cosmic reality in the light of a hypothesis presented by history or a tradition can systematically prevent young people from making false starts" (*The Risk of Education*, 57). As we are initiated into Christian life, we discover that to be human is to be created in the image and likeness of God and thus oriented toward community. We learn that the happy life is not a matter of grasping and seizing power but an apprenticeship in the art of self-emptying love. We discover that God has a preferential option for the least of these. These are hypotheses that make sense of what it means to be human in the world—hypotheses that are challenging for the adolescent and the adult alike!

But, it's not enough to present these hypotheses and demand that the person accept them. That's not education—it's indoctrination. The risk of education is that we must invite each person to verify these truths in his or her own life:

> Even a clear presentation of the meaning of things and the real,
> intense authority of the education is insufficient to meet the
> needs of the adolescent. He must instead be stimulated to *person-*
> *ally confront his own origin*. This means that the student must
> verify the traditional contents being offered to him, which can
> be done only if he himself *takes the initiative*: no one else can do
> it for him. (Giussani, *The Risk of Education*, 67)

Persons receiving a Christian education grounded in freedom
need to practice a life that has become attuned to Christ's. They
will need to compare what they discover in the hypothesis of the
church's proclamation with the experience of being human. They
will need to do so not under the compulsion of the educator who
holds out a sacramental stick but through giving their lives over
to this act of verification. They'll have to take the risk of asking,
"Is it true? And if it is, how will that change everything?"

The individual is provoked, encounters the hypothesis, and verifies the truth of the hypothesis in his or her life through the church.
For Giussani, the church is the place of friendship with Christ and
one another. It is the concrete space in time and history where we
encounter the risen Lord through the community of disciples. Defining the formative quality of the church, Giussani states:

> The great dwelling place that is the Church becomes flesh, is
> realized in capillary terminals . . . in which it becomes present
> in every place, chosen beforehand by God's plan. The great
> dwelling place that is the Church is realized inside homes, the
> dwelling places that are the concentration, the coalescence of her
> life in a day-to-day dimension of time and space. (Giussani, Al-
> berto, and Prades, *Generating Traces in the History of the World*, 73)

Christian formation includes friendship with those Christians who
have been provoked by the mystery of Christ. It is a community
of disciples, called the church, who have become a living sign of
the church's hypothesis. It is a community that verifies, incom-
pletely of course, the reality that God is the meaning of life. And
because we know this meaning, we live in the family of God in a

way that witnesses to the presence of God's love in our families, friendships, workplaces, and the public sphere.

For Giussani, this threefold approach of provocation, hypothesis, and verification is the privileged way that Christianity can be taught in our own age. It is passed on through not only a textbook or a video series but an encounter with Jesus Christ through the mystery of the church. This encounter does not leave behind the deepest desires of the human heart but takes them up: "God *wants* to pass through the humanity of all those he has taken hold of in Baptism" (Giussani, *Why the Church?*, 126–27).

Giussani's approach to formation is similar to the RCIA's. The catechumenate is a journey in which one is provoked to initial conversion, to a progression in faith throughout the catechumenate, to receiving the sacraments of initiation in which the mystery of Christ is now verified in one's very body (RCIA 6). Throughout the process, one is accompanied by the entire community of the church, who themselves join "the catechumens in reflecting on the value of the paschal mystery and by renewing their own conversion, the faithful provide an example that will help the catechumens to obey the Holy Spirit more generously" (RCIA 4).

Liturgical formation in the RCIA is not merely about the catechumens and candidates. It is the re-formation of the desires of the whole community of believers to verify the radical hypothesis that has brought us together into one: "Beloved, let us love one another, because love is of God; everyone who loves is begotten by God and knows God. Whoever is without love does not know God, for God is love" (1 John 4:7-8). If we believe that God is love, that this love is available to us in parish churches throughout the world, if we verify this love in our very lives, we will find ourselves living out the worshipful wisdom that Christ has provided for the salvation of the world.

Liturgical Formation in the RCIA

The journey of the RCIA is permeated with liturgical formation. Everyone who has been involved in the process knows this.

Who can forget their first Easter Vigil as the elect were plunged into the water of salvation? The new Christian is led from the earliest stages of faith awakened through the church's worship to participating as baptized, confirmed, and eucharistized sons and daughters of the triune God. Liturgical rites function as efficacious moments in which one's identity is formed. After initiation, the process of mystagogy is not concerned only with "explaining" what took place in the rites. Instead, one is to be led more deeply into the mystery of Christ that unfolds through the liturgical year. The rest of Christian life becomes an echoing of this mystery as lived in day-to-day life.

Liturgical formation is thus essential to the RCIA throughout the process. In this book, written for those engaged in the pastoral practice of RCIA, we will undertake a deeper inquiry into the nature of liturgical formation in the act of initiating Christians. The book will consider the specific liturgical rites of the RCIA, the formative nature of the eucharistic assembly, and the manner in which liturgical practice spills over into the domestic sphere.

The book centers around Giussani's threefold pedagogy of provocation, hypothesis, and verification. The goal of this examination is not a deeper reading of Giussani's work. These three moments of education assist the pastoral minister in thinking through the purpose of liturgical formation. Liturgy provokes, it offers a hypothesis about the ultimate meaning of life grounded in Christ, and it is a moment in which our life in Christ is verified through sacramental practice.

Each time the church prays the liturgy, these three moments of provocation, hypothesis, and verification are assumed. But for the sake of helping us think through liturgical formation in the RCIA, I will develop a model in which the following occur:

1. Liturgical provocation is the privileged educational approach of pre-evangelization and inquiry.

2. Liturgical hypothesis is the privileged educational approach of the catechumenate.

3. Liturgical verification is the privileged educational approach of the period of purification and enlightenment, culminating in the celebration of the Easter Vigil.

4. Mystagogy is a re-presentation of the liturgical mystery of the church that provokes, offers a new hypothesis, and involves practices for verification.

Chapter 1 of this book will take up liturgical prayer as a moment of provocation. The chapter will analyze six dimensions of late modern life that stops the process of questioning for the catechumen: a thin sense of God, a rugged individualism, an overemphasis on technology as salvation, a loss of wonder, a throwaway culture that bypasses the dignity of the human person, and the "liturgy" of consumerism. The church's liturgy should provoke one to see the reality of God, of life in communion, of the need for a salvation that emerges outside of ourselves, of beauty, of the intrinsic dignity of the human being made for worship, and of the nature of the world as gift. The liturgy should function as this moment of provocation for every person, especially those who are first inquiring into the nature of Christian life with one another. The chapter also argues that this "moment" of the RCIA requires non-eucharistic liturgical celebrations (adapted versions of the Liturgy of the Hours) where an evangelizing provocation can unfold in each of our parishes. Such liturgies must be celebrated not by the RCIA group alone but by the whole parish. Finally, this chapter shows how the rite of entrance into the catechumenate now transforms the inquirers (now catechumens) into occasions for provocation for the entire church. The required dismissal of the catechumens solidifies this moment of provocation for the assembly and the catechumens alike.

Chapter 2 of this book will take up the pedagogy of liturgical hypothesis for the catechumenate. During the period of the catechumenate, the goal is to move the catechumen from liturgical provocation to a reasonable account of the liturgical life of the church. Reason here does not mean scientific inquiry. Instead, it is the process whereby we begin to make sense of the "really" real through the church's practices of worship. The chapter begins by looking at some of the rites ascribed to the catechumenate, including celebrations of the Liturgy of the Word, blessings, and exorcisms. These liturgical rites are not optional but emphasize that all catechesis in the catechumenate should function as an occasion of offering a liturgical hypothesis for human life.

This chapter also argues that such a process of liturgical formation requires an initial familiarity with the signs and embodied practices of worship. It is liturgical competency. Such competency is akin to a pianist first learning where middle-C is, what posture to assume while playing piano, and how to play chords rather than simply melody. The basics matter. And we have to do a better job of teaching these basics in the RCIA itself rather than just presuming that everyone will pick them up on their own.

The catechumenate is also concerned with a deeper understanding of the liturgical and sacramental life of the church. Just as musical competency leads to the study of music theory, so too we move from liturgical competency to a deeper study of what we're doing in the act of worship. The core rites and sacraments of the church must be taught in a way that the contemporary person sees them as the gifts that they are. The rites and sacraments of the church should be taught as a hypothesis for the deepest desires of the human heart.

Chapter 3 of this book deals with the pedagogy of liturgical verification. It begins with a close examination of the Rite of Election, or enrollment, as a privileged moment of verification. The catechumen now becomes the elect, preparing for the Gospel to be written upon one's body. The chapter then looks closely at how this verification plays out in the scrutinies during the Third, Fourth, and Fifth Sundays of Lent; the handing-over (*traditio*) and giving back (*redditio*) of the Creed; the presentation of the Lord's Prayer; and preparation rites for Holy Saturday. The chapter shows how the rites of the Easter Vigil are the supreme moment of liturgical verification in which through the sacraments of initiation the elect become priests, prophets, and royal figures through the rich efficacy of the signs of this dazzling night.

The fourth and final chapter takes up the period of mystagogy. The chapter begins by focusing on some ways that mystagogy may be practiced as a way of inviting the neophytes to reflect on their experience of the Easter Vigil, learning to meditate on the wisdom that they celebrated in the liturgy itself. But, the chapter further argues that mystagogy will only be effective during the season of Easter if the parish practices mystagogy throughout the liturgical year.

Finally, a note about this book. The book presumes that the RCIA is oriented toward the initiation of unbaptized Christians. Such a presumption is not evident in many parishes, where those seeking fuller communion in the Catholic Church are often inappropriately initiated at the Easter Vigil. Christians seeking full communion with the Catholic Church should be able to enter during any season of the liturgical year. Yet, in practice it often makes sense, at least from the perspective of pastoral resources, to do a similar formation with baptized Christians and catechumens. For this reason, after chapter 3, I will provide a brief excursus on the role of liturgical formation in receiving those seeking full communion with the Catholic Church. Nonetheless, where the book speaks about the nature of liturgical formation with catechumens, it can be presumed that the insights are true of all human beings whether they are inquirers, catechumens, those seeking full communion with the Catholic Church, or Catholics reared in holy mother church from their very first breath of life.

This book is dedicated to Maxwell Johnson, professor of liturgical and sacramental theology at the University of Notre Dame. It was in a liturgical history course with Dr. Johnson during my senior year that I discovered what constituted a mature approach to liturgical formation. His commitment to a retrieval of a deep understanding of liturgical history, of a proper celebration of the rites of initiation, and his commitment to ecumenism has been formative to my identity. Any insights in this book are the result of the sophisticated formation he has provided his students in the art of living liturgically. Any deficits are my own.

Chapter 1

Liturgical Formation in the Precatechumenate

Students entered the auditorium, attending a talk on *The Saint John's Bible*—a lecture that the professor (yours truly!) assigned for extra credit. Many of them had grown up with the Scriptures in their homes. Some had read and prayed with the Bible in the context of the family or in youth groups. Others had a copy of the Good Book somewhere in the home, perhaps on the shelf of a family room. Not a few of these students were reading the Bible for the first time in the context of a theology course at the University of Notre Dame. No matter the background, each of the students had grown up with the Bible as "another book" that could be placed on a shelf. While most thought that the text of the Scriptures were inspired or at least quite important for Western history, they grew up with the assumption that the Bible (at least in terms of production) is like other books.

Over the course of the hour, their relationship with the Bible changed. *The Saint John's Bible* is a handwritten, illuminated copy of the Scriptures, created by a team of scribes throughout the world, led by the artist Donald Jackson. It was Donald Jackson's dream, even as a young artist, to produce a handwritten copy of the entire Bible.

The kick-off lecturer led the gathered crowd in a tour of *The Saint John's Bible.* They learned about the art of calligraphy, the vellum used as the pages of the Bible, and the history of the ink that the scribes employed in copying the Scriptures. Many attendees were interested in the illuminations that decorated page after page of the Scriptures from the opening page of Genesis to the closing chapter of Revelation.

At the end of the lecture, they gathered at the entrance of the auditorium, approaching the volume of the gospels. Fifty or so students huddled around *The Saint John's Bible,* waiting for the text to be opened. As the lecturer opened the book to the first page of the Gospel of Matthew, there was an audible gasp. In brilliant red and gold was a menorah, illuminating the genealogy of Jesus Christ. A chapter of the Bible that had previously meant nothing to the students, listing the genealogy of "Jesus Christ, the son of David, the son of Abraham" (Matt 1:1), provoked questions from the students. What were the various names written in Greek, Hebrew, and Aramaic? Why did the artist choose to decorate the opening chapter in this manner, using a menorah? Why would someone devote so much attention, so much care to a single chapter of the Bible?

The next day in class, I asked the students what they thought about the Bible. They told me that they couldn't believe that someone would spend so much time, so much money, *so much* in creating this piece of art. They found themselves provoked, wondering what this meant about their own relationship to the Bible. If Donald Jackson (and before him countless professional scribes and monks) found this text so important, maybe there really was something here in the Scriptures worth looking at.

A Second Look

All across the world, people know about Christianity. They know something about the Catholic Church. Even if they're not experts in doctrine or practice, they know that Catholics have a pope. They know that Catholics go to Mass. They may have an image of dimly lit churches with lots of candles, statues, processions, and incense.

Yet as every teacher has learned, knowing something is often far worse than knowing nothing. If I know nothing about baseball except that it is a game where people hit balls with bats and run in a circle, it may explain why I find the game useless. To really know baseball, to savor it, I may need to be open to that which I don't know. I would need to give baseball a second look. I might need to attend a game, experiencing baseball not as a virtual event on television but in the flesh—to smell the odors of the ballpark, all the while savoring the experience of a sun-splashed summer day in the bleachers at Fenway Park.

The process of evangelization or the precatechumenate in the RCIA invites men and women to take a second look at the church. As the rite clarifies, the purpose of this stage of evangelization is the conversion of men and women, who although not yet Christians encounter the living God in the person of Jesus Christ and "commit themselves sincerely to him. For he who is the way, the truth, and the life fulfills all their spiritual expectations, indeed infinitely surpasses them" (RCIA 36). The precatechumenate facilitates a conversion "so that the genuine will to follow Christ and seek baptism may mature" (RCIA 37). This period of the RCIA is not a way of finding more space in a curriculum to teach particular doctrines or practices. It's not like the drop/add period that takes place early in a college semester, whereby students can determine if they like the professor or the course material enough to continue. The period of evangelization and the precatechumenate is the time to provoke men and women to become disciples.

The liturgical life of the church is integral to this process of evangelization. But, in many ministerial circles, it is not uncommon to hear that men and women must *first* be invited into a personal relationship with Jesus Christ before they discover the fruitfulness of life in the church. We should preach Jesus, not the church, they say. After meeting Jesus, they'll learn to love the liturgy, studying Christian doctrine, and caring for the poor.

There is a truth to this claim. If we treat the church as a repository of abstract ideas or required practices, it's a problem. The church does not offer a thesis to the world like a philosophical school but provides a space to encounter the person of Jesus Christ. Catholicism is an event in which men and women throughout the world meet the risen Lord.

At the same time, if we radically separate Jesus and the church, it's also a problem. The scandal of the cross is that Jesus Christ comes to us through the human words of the Scriptures, through the prayerful rites of the church, through the communion of love shared among the faithful, and through the immigrant who suffers the results of political power. As John Henry Newman preached in his sermon "Christ Hidden from the World" to students and faculty at Oxford, "The Church is called 'His Body': what his material Body was when He was visible on earth, such is the Church now" (*Parochial and Plain Sermons*). To encounter the risen Lord means that we must come to know his hidden presence in the church.

We must invite individuals to take a second look at the mystery of the church as a way of coming to know the person of Jesus Christ. The doctrines that we teach, the stories that we tell, the practices that form us into God's family reveal in a hidden and wonderful way the presence of Jesus Christ operating in the world today.

For this reason, liturgical evangelization is not an oxymoron. Evangelization is not reducible to one-on-one ministry or small groups, even if it will necessarily include such encounters. Liturgical evangelization is part of an approach to missionary discipleship that focuses on the basics. As Pope Francis describes in The Joy of the Gospel, the charter of evangelization in our age: "When we adopt a pastoral goal and a missionary style which would actually reach everyone without exception or exclusion, the message has to concentrate on the essentials, on what is most beautiful, most grand, most appealing, and the same time most necessary" (35).

During the stage of evangelization and the catechumenate, the seeker should slowly be attuned to the way that the church's public prayer, her liturgy, is necessary to following Jesus. This doesn't mean inducing guilt in those seeking to enter the church (you know, to be saved, you really need to go to Mass every week). Instead, we need to invite people to participate in the liturgy in our parishes. We need to say to those budding followers of Jesus, come and see. Come and take a second look at the wondrous mystery of love that we celebrate at our parishes every day of the week!

Liturgical Evangelization as Celebration

If we're going to invite seekers to come meet the risen Lord in our parishes, the first step is to make sure that everyone else in the parish is aware that the risen Lord is in fact present in our parish. As a theologian, I spend a lot of time traveling around the world. This means that I'm often away from home on Sundays, looking for a place to worship God wherever I find myself. The good news is that I can often find a Mass, one in which I'm not the youngest person in the church. The bad news is that so many of our parish liturgical celebrations are sometimes without joy, devoid of hospitality, closed to everyone except the local intelligentsia who know what is happening.

Friends of mine once attended a Mass in the Archdiocese of Boston. It was St. Patrick's Day in a parish in the North End. A Saturday Vigil Mass, there was no music. And the cantor welcomed them into the celebration of Christ's sacrificial love by pronouncing at the beginning of Mass, "Welcome, outsiders!"

This New England "welcome" is extreme. But imagine that my visiting, very Catholic friends in Boston had stepped into that church for the very first time not as Catholics but as seekers. Perhaps they had just lost their father and were turning to the church for comfort. Perhaps they were struggling with their marriage and had turned to God in their suffering. Perhaps they had just welcomed a child into their lives and wanted, in some small way, to offer thanksgiving to the God whom they had come to recognize through the joy of a new child. The religious conversion begins with the great perhaps.

The Sunday Mass at parishes and college campus ministries throughout the United States remains a privileged space for evangelization. It's one of the few places that a seeker can show up without committing to the whole thing. A seeker can sneak in the back, try to blend in with the other worshipers, and perhaps experience God in the process. This is precisely what both Thomas Merton and Dorothy Day did in New York City. It was part of their own evangelization. They entered into these churches and discovered a presence, a love, call it a "mystery," that made sense of everything else they were experiencing in their lives.

The parish "evangelizes" in its celebration of the rites of the church. It evangelizes through celebration. The connotations of the English word "celebration" do not sufficiently communicate what the Latin *celebratio* means. The church's "celebration" of the Passover of Jesus Christ from death to new life, of humanity's participation in this mystery of love, isn't a birthday or anniversary party. *Celebratio* points to a large gathering of people, a public act of praise and commendation, or a festival with a large number of persons in attendance. The liturgy is a celebration not because it's always happy, always full of what we consider good news like winning the lottery or a national championship. It is a celebration because it is a public space where the world can partake in the festive news that love unto the end, divine love, is the meaning of the world. The liturgy is the most serious of all celebrations.

The liturgy thus evangelizes because men and women are invited into the festivities of the once dead and now risen and living Lord. Seekers should see on the faces of their fellow worshipers not ecstatic happiness but real joy. Joy that comes from the good news that life has conquered death. In the great battle between power and love, God's love wins! Every dimension of our humanity is meant to be redeemed through the power of Christ.

That's why the liturgy should be full of song. That's why our preaching should sound like a victory proclamation instead of a dreadful catalogue of dos and don'ts. That's why our churches are meant to be beautiful spaces that fill every one of the senses with wonder. The *celebratio* taking place in each parish is the redemption of humanity through the glorification of God.

The nature of the liturgy as *celebratio* does not mean that a Sunday morning Eucharist at our parish must be filled with artificially happy people. It's good to introduce oneself to newcomers in the parish, asking their names and welcoming them into prayer. But it's dreadfully artificial to say that Mass *must* begin by asking everyone present to stand up, turn around, and greet one's neighbor. That's inauthentic. Many of those in the parish come to the liturgy with wounded hearts, with sorrows that they are offering up to God in love. The *celebratio* of the liturgy means that even our sorrows can be healed through the loving balm of Jesus Christ. Liturgy gives people space to enter into divine love within the communion of faith without erasing their freedom.

I'll always remember the Mass that I attended in Belgium after receiving word that my grandmother had suffered a terminal stroke caused by her Alzheimer's. I entered the sparsely attended Vigil Mass in the cathedral. The Mass was celebrated in French. While my French is good enough for reading, my aural comprehension is so-so. I thus sat in silence. The music was unfamiliar to me. But the familiar ritual of kneeling and standing, of crossing myself and gazing up at the presence of Jesus Christ, was comforting to me. Exchanging the sign of peace with my fellow pilgrims was a source of deep comfort. There was no artificiality to the celebration, to the very real communion that I shared with God and neighbor that late afternoon. My time at Mass was a way for me to find a little space in a foreign city where for a moment I could offer my own sorrow to God, aware that Jesus Christ and the entire communion of saints would share it with me. I walked away from the cathedral that day, a stranger among strangers, nonetheless full of joyous hope.

The privileged locus of evangelization for each and every parish is the regular, beautiful, faithfully prayed liturgy of the church. It is the place where the long-time Catholic and the seeker may come and discover the risen Lord working in the midst of God's people. As the Constitution on the Sacred Liturgy at the Second Vatican Council noted, "the liturgy, through which 'the work of our redemption takes place,' . . . is supremely effective in enabling the faithful to express in their lives and portray to others the mystery of Christ and the real nature of the true church" (2). If we want to have parishes that are evangelizing, we better have really good liturgical celebrations.

Good Liturgy Is Provocative

But what constitutes good liturgy? If you're familiar with battles among liturgists, you may be tempted to stop reading this book immediately! The question of good liturgy can be neuralgic. The person who loves smells and bells despises guitars and banners. The lover of Haugen and Haas hates Palestrina and Tallis. Entering into these battles, I often think about the words that Dante encounters as he passes through the gates of hell, "Abandon hope, all ye who enter here."

But, fearful reader, read on. This book will not be an occasion for another round of liturgical wars. This is not because I don't think there is such a thing as good liturgy. There is, and I'll define it below. Instead, it's because I believe that there are a variety of possibilities for good liturgy when you get the definition right.

What do I mean by good liturgy? To answer this question, let's start with what good liturgy isn't. Good liturgy doesn't change the words and structure of the Mass so that the priest can prove to his local ordinary and assembly that he's not afraid of following his own drummer. Nor is good liturgy an aesthetic performance where the focus is on the quality of the choir, the glory of the architectural space, and the splendor of the vestments. Good liturgy doesn't mean that everyone in the parish takes a turn as communion minister and lector. It also doesn't mean total silence and absolute formality reign all the time. In each of these cases, the focus of the liturgy is on the liturgical performance rather than on the purpose of the liturgy: the glorification of God and the sanctification of humanity.

Good liturgy glorifies God and sanctifies the human person. You can't separate the two moments. In the liturgy, we bring every dimension of our humanity into the act of worship. At Sunday Mass, I don't go to my parish church as a God-glorifier while leaving behind my identity as a husband, father, friend, and teacher. I am a human being whose vocation is the glorification of God and who carries out this glorification through my identity as a husband, father, friend, and teacher. At the same time, the focus of the eucharistic liturgy is not on my identity. We don't enter into Mass, hearing hymns that talk just about my situation, my identity, or my preferred cultural group. I enter into the church's act of sacrificial praise to the Father, the Son, and the Holy Spirit. I arrive as I am, and in the act of worshiping, I place my identity in a larger story—the narrative in which the triune God has redeemed the human family.

Good liturgy gives the necessary space for the process of sanctification to unfold in the lives of each member of Christ's Body, the church. And it does so because such liturgy places the mystery of divine love at the center of the activity. For example, at Christmas, lots of folks come back to church who haven't been in a while. Sons and daughters of active parishioners travel in, attending midnight Mass in an almost nostalgic manner. They enter into the celebration of Christmas perhaps with some anxiety, as they restore relationships with family members they haven't seen in a while. In our parishes, there are some who struggle with Christmas. They're lonely, suffering from the death of a spouse or a dear friend. Christmas is a *celebratio* in which Jesus Christ, the Word made flesh, takes up all these aspects of the human condition. On the feast of Christmas, we wondrously celebrate that the Word, the very Creator of the world, took flesh and dwelt among us as an infant. The Word became speechless. And therefore, God can enter into every aspect of what it means to be human, raising it up to be transfigured through the radiance of love.

A good Christmas liturgy places this mystery of love at its center. It may include polyphony like *O Magnum Mysterium* or the hymn *Silent Night*. The organ may be used along with mariachi music. Whatever music is used in the liturgy, it should allow the mystery of love be given expression through songs of praise and joy. The Mass will include ample silence for the assembly to reflect on the wonder of the mystery. The presider will not rush through

Mass but invite the assembly to contemplate what has taken place at Christmas. There will be joy among the assembly, not just because Christmas is a feast, but because God has dwelt among us in the most intimate of ways, taking up our flesh. Liturgists must begin from this wondrous mystery, from this divine provocation, if the liturgy is to be good.

Good liturgy is provocative. It provokes from us mortals a response of wonder before the God who is love. The wonder that we experience does not leave us paralyzed with fear. We enter into this mystery, aware that the God who became infant wants every part of our humanity to become a space where the Word can become flesh and dwell among us. There is something for us to do—to give ourselves over to this process of sanctification. Good liturgy creates space for God to act, to enter into our history once more in love.

If we want evangelizing liturgies, the ones that will attract seekers from off the street, celebrating good, "provocative" liturgies are key—liturgies that place at the center God's salvific activity rather than the priest, the choir, or the assembly. It is precisely this kind of liturgy that will lead seekers to take a second look at the church.

Provoked: What Next?

In the following chapters, the reader will have more opportunities to think about what happens in the act of liturgy and why it's evangelizing for everyone from seekers to mature Catholics. But since this chapter is focusing on the stage of evangelization and the precatechumenate, what happens when these seekers find themselves provoked by the church's worship? How do we lead these inquirers into a deeper understanding of what is happening in the liturgy? How can we bring these new Christians into the practice of radical discipleship that the liturgy teaches?

In his important trilogy on "cultural liturgies," the Reformed Christian philosopher James K.A. Smith describes the process by which modern culture forms us into certain assumptions or postures toward life. When seekers or inquirers enter into our churches, we have to remember that, while they are not natives to

Catholic liturgy, they have been formed through various cultural practices or stories that are part of day-to-day life. They have been worshiping something or someone before they have darkened the doors of our churches.

I've often discovered this fact, especially around the time that RCIA groups I've participated in discuss Catholic social teaching. When our RCIA community begins to discuss the common good, solidarity, human dignity, and the preferential option for the poor, catechumens bristle. Formed in a political world shaped by Republicans and Democrats, they presume that Catholic social teaching will align with one party or the other. They have been educated for polarization through the annual cycle of debates and elections. And they often find it challenging to discover that the church upholds the dignity of the unborn, the undocumented immigrant, and the prisoner on death row. There is something pushing them away from recognizing the wisdom of Catholic social teaching because everything they've ever learned about society and politics has been mediated through ritual blaming performed on cable news.

Just as political partisanship and polarization is an obstacle to encountering the wisdom of Catholic social teaching, many of those seeking Jesus Christ in the Catholic Church have their own difficulties entering into fruitful worship. They find themselves distracted or confused about what is happening. They need good mentorship from a more mature Catholic to guide them through the process of worshipful wisdom. They confuse the mundane gift of weekly worship for boredom, expecting constant affections rather than slow attunement to divine life. They take these signs as evidence that the Christian life isn't working, that it's time to look elsewhere for a hypothesis.

Thus, those involved in running the RCIA process, as well as the entire pastoral team, have to function like doctors. They have to diagnose where our false assumptions about the nature of worship make it harder to adore the living God. Having worked with adolescents, undergraduates, and adults over the last eight years, I have learned that the primary malaises we bring to the act of worship include a thin sense of God, individualism, a hope that technology will save, a loss of wonder, a throwaway culture, and the liturgy of consumerism.

The Malaises That Inhibit Worship

The Absent God

The sociologist Christian Smith has analyzed the presumed religion of most Americans. He calls this religion Moralistic Therapeutic Deism. Americans often believe in a God who exists somewhere out there, who gets involved in our lives when we're interested that this God be involved, but who happily doesn't ask too much from us. If we're nice and decent, not shoving people into doors, then we all go to heaven where we'll hang out together. This is the kind of God that politicians invoke at public events, asking that this "God" bless America.

Many of my students are at least "kind of" Moralistic Therapeutic Deists. They're happy to have God operating on the outside of their lives as a divine butler who intervenes when asked. They assume that one should be a decent person, and they find folks who engage in terrible behavior abhorrent (probably bound for something like a really boring hell). They don't actively deny the existence of God, but they also don't allow this God to influence key decisions about work, family, politics, or leisure time.

For this reason, they also think that worship is a matter of "begging" for this God to pay some attention to their lives when it's necessary to do so. We go to Mass or we engage in private devotions because we hope that this God will let me into college, heal my mother from her illness, and let me find my spouse. If these things don't happen, it is assumed that God isn't real or just doesn't listen to our deepest problems. If a budding Christian comes to Mass on a weekly basis, hoping that God will finally intervene in a situation involving the sickness of a loved one only to discover the disappointment of continued illness or death, they could easily walk away. They could come to the conclusion that God doesn't care. God doesn't exist.

Mature Christians, of course, know better. We know that the God we worship is so radically involved in our lives that "he humbled himself, becoming obedient to death, even death on a cross" (Phil 2:8). Our God is the one who entered into the history of Israel, choosing this nation among all nations to be God's own. Our God is the one who became flesh, entering into friendship with humankind. Our God is the one who freely gave himself on the cross, loving us unto the end. Our God is love.

"Rugged" Individualism

Moralistic Therapeutic Deism is not the only problem that many of our fledgling Christians struggle with. For some, worshiping in a community is also a difficulty. Immature Christians could imagine that the act of worship should be a radically individual experience—one in which the entire created order disappears except for God and me. Everyone else is a distraction, moving me away from the mystical encounter that is my destiny.

As a parent with two young children, I often encounter this malaise. Once, my baptized son, then three years old, was not being especially reverent during the celebration of the Eucharist. He was jumping up and down on the pew during Mass, creating a scene that we were attempting to quell, using our powers of parental persuasion. But, you know three-year-olds. The woman in the pew behind me kindly asked that we leave the Mass because she was trying to pray and could not because of the presence of our son. In her imagination, liturgical prayer was a private encounter with God in which every possible annoyance should be eliminated. The liturgy was a moment in which the individual person, the self, experiences an encounter of love apart from the rest of the community.

Now, it is more than reasonable to take a three-year-old out of Mass if he's being especially irreverent, screaming at the top of his lungs to escape. I have often been the parent dragging my son to the back of the church when he has passed beyond the bounds of acceptable human behavior. As a member of Christ's

Body, I'm aware that there are many men and women attending the liturgy seeking to encounter the living God, who enters into their lives with a love that no human being can imagine. I want to foster this encounter. Leaving with my son or daughter is part of my act of worship, my contribution to the community on a particular Sunday.

But part of this encounter is through the assembly of Christ's Body including young children struggling to behave, members of Christ's Body singing out of tune, and the regular assembly who are on pilgrimage toward holiness. This radical belonging to Christ's Body, such that my neighbor becomes part of my deepest concern, is integral to Christian salvation. We are not saved as individuals alone. As Pope Francis has written, "We are never completely ourselves unless we belong to a people. That is why no one is saved alone, as an isolated individual. Rather, God draws us to himself, taking into account the complex fabric of interpersonal relationships present in a human community. God wanted to enter into the life and history of a people" (Rejoice and Be Glad, 6).

This claim goes against the primary assumption that many bring into the religious act—that salvation is about the cultivation of a spiritual self, of my "personal" and thus "individual" spirituality. Liturgical prayer, of course, recognizes that there is an individual personality that participates in the liturgy. That's why good liturgy should leave space for the entire catalogue of human affections— praise, adoration, lament, silence, and wonder. But I don't go to Mass or the Liturgy of the Hours because it "resonates" with my individual spirituality. I go because through baptism, confirmation, and the Eucharist, I have been initiated into Christ's Body. I go because when I'm in attendance (even if I'm in the narthex letting my one-year-old walk around), I'm acknowledging that my body, my life, my whole existence is not my own. It is Christ's. It is a self who discovers his deepest identity in the church, in the communion of believers who celebrate the festival of the Lamb once slain. The end of Christian life is not reducible to the salvation of the individual human being but the transformation of the whole world, starting with this parish, into a space of love.

Technology as Salvation

Some years ago, the University of Notre Dame hosted a forum on the crisis precipitated by climate change. At the event, engineers made suggestions about the role that technological innovation could play in saving the planet from destruction. Such technological interventions ranged from the creation of biodegradable packaging for food to the making of new sources of renewable energy.

One of the engineers on the panel revealed a problem with the plan. A prominent snack food company created biodegradable packaging for chips. But the packaging made an annoying noise when customers opened up the bag. Because of this noise, the customers rejected the packaging, causing the company to switch back to the older packaging. The engineer noted that while technological innovation could be used to help the planet, something more is needed. Human beings have to want to change. They'd have to change their own habits of consumption if the planet has a chance to survive.

This narrative provides an image for understanding the third malaise under examination: a false sense of the salvific possibilities of technology. Now before proceeding, it is essential to underline two things. First, I am not saying all technology is bad. I don't avoid iPhones or computers as if they are the plague. I don't sit in public places, bemoaning the sins of the young who spend so much time on screens. Such technology is part of my day-to-day life too. And this technology is often very helpful, enabling me to keep in touch with scholars and ministers around the globe. Second, I'm appreciative that technology has led to a number of gifts to human life in the last century. Because of technological innovation in the creation of medicine, for example, when my son gets an ear infection, we're not worried that this might be the disease that will end his life.

What I'm worried about is the assumption that everything in our lives can be solved through technological innovation. If only we had better computers, dating apps, ways to produce energy, mobile phones, and transportation, then human beings will finally be happy. People will form connections that last a lifetime, find a spouse, be able to use energy without any effect on the environment, create videos of every experience, and be able to develop nearly infinite mobility.

Now, very few people would profess such a credo to us at least using these exact words. But, it's possible to look at advertising to see how this dynamic plays out. Several years ago, Apple produced a commercial for Christmas showing a video of a young man visiting his family but never looking up from his phone. At the end of the commercial, the young man presented to his family why he was gazing with almost iconic devotion to his phone—he was making a video that documented every dimension of his family's celebration of Christmas. The commercial, most likely directed to parents of teens obsessed with devices, performs an act of persuasion. If every parent purchases a phone for their child, there will be the possibility of a renewed human relationship. Buy this phone. Save the relationship.

What does this hope have to do with liturgy? Our adoration of technology must not be understood as a clash between adoring the transcendent God of Catholicism versus worshiping at the altar of immanent technology. Rather, the problem is that technology itself taps into our desire for transcendence, for a source of salvation outside of ourselves. The hope that we might be saved through the creation of the next novel device functions almost likes a religion. Think about what happens when you look at your phone, checking for a new e-mail message or a notification from Instagram. There is a sense of euphoric delight. Someone has connected with me. We grow addicted to this encounter, gazing with frequency at our phone. We hope that another message will appear on our phone, that another connection will be made.

The smartphone is therefore a rival to authentic worship. For in the act of worship, we await the coming of the triune God into history. It is not technological innovation that will save but the love of God that has shaped the past, becomes present in our world here and now, and will be with us into the future. We are saved through a personal encounter with Jesus Christ—the one who came as an infant, who comes this very day through the proclamation of the Scriptures and in his eucharistic presence, and who will come at the end of time to judge the living and the dead. This encounter is mediated not through sophisticated chips and shaped glass but through the materiality of water, bread, wine, book, and oil.

The boredom that so many people experience in worship is caused by this misplaced hope that technology will provide an interminable answer to our desire. But divine worship cultivates a radically different hope: that the insatiability of our desire is not soothed through innovation but the eternal, ever-present, ever-coming Lord of the universe.

Loss of Wonder

The nearly universal presence of technology in our lives has also changed the way that we encounter the world. Growing up, I would go on lengthy hikes in the mountains of East Tennessee. Climbing to the top of a peak, I would be struck by the beauty of the foothills of the Great Smoky Mountains. In the summer, I would contemplate the lush greenery of the Appalachian Mountains. I'd take the same hike in the fall, encountering a fiery palette of red, orange, and yellow. During each of these hikes, I found myself wondering at the beauty of the created order, sitting in silence on a rocky hilltop. While hiking, I'd often sit at the top of the peak for hours—journaling, thinking about the great questions that occupied the attention of my adolescent or young adult self. Hiking allowed me not only to encounter the *wonderful* quality of creation, but to encounter the wonder of existence itself. Who made me? What did I hope for out of life? Was I in love with her?

Since I purchased my smartphone eight years ago, my experience of hiking has changed. I still love the mountains, the silence that falls over me as I ascend the trail. But when I reach the top of the trail, rather than sit in silence, I begin to "curate" the experience. I try to find the best picture to take that I'll later send out to followers on Instagram, Twitter, and Facebook. I'll attempt to take a "selfie," one that shows evidence of my rugged hike but still makes me look like a handsome hiker. I'll search for a signal from a roving tower, hoping that I can send pictures out to my family, friends, and #CatholicTwitter. Where there is no signal, I'll move down the mountain as quickly as possible, looking to reconnect to the digital world through my phone.

Wonder, as a human experience, is not reducible to being overwhelmed by beauty. Wonder is also an openness to meditation, to asking great questions that are written in the human heart. Looking out over the Grand Canyon, I wonder at the sublime beauty of creation. But I also "wonder" when I engage in practices of reflection, not just as an individual but with a community of fellow inquirers. Some of the best conversations I've had with my spouse were on hikes or in isolated places where we were able to talk to one another without interruption.

Many of the undergraduates whom I work with are losing this capacity for wonder. I look up at the beginning of class and see everyone's eyes are focused on their smartphones. They don't talk to one another but sit as isolated monads. Because they're so concerned about "curating a self," they're often unwilling to ask the great questions that matter in life. From a young age, they have been told that success in life is what matters, and the way to achieve this success is through an education that enables them to get good jobs. They think they know who they are, what they need, and are pursuing an education to receive the credentials that will allow them to be successful. Many of them suffer from anxiety, caused by a mixture of perpetual activity, unrealistic expectations about what constitutes human happiness, and a sense that their lives are not their own.

Still, they hunger for isolated spaces where they can separate themselves from the constant notifications provided by technological devices. They want to spend time together in conversation and prayer, apart from the noise of life. They want to be around that which is beautiful, to encounter something that raises in them the great questions that each human being will eventually have to answer.

In other words, this loss of wonder can be healed through creating spaces of wonder through the liturgy. But we in the church are just as likely to allow the efficiency of modern life to intrude on our act of worship. We rush through prayers, homilies, and sermons— giving no one a chance to think. Presiders fill the liturgy with words upon words, refusing to let a moment of silence blossom in a desert of verbosity. We, in the church, have to ask why we seem to be so afraid to create these spaces of wonder that may provoke both mature and developing Christians to desire God anew.

Throwaway Culture

In his preaching, Pope Francis often characterizes modern society as a "throwaway culture." Human beings have been created with dignity by God. They are part of a whole ecology of creation. But a throwaway culture puts too much emphasis on the power of human beings to shape the world according to their own desires. This emphasis on human power to do whatever it wants is deadly not just for the environment but for our call to solidarity with our fellow human beings. He writes in *Laudato Si'*: On Care for Our Common Home:

> When we fail to acknowledge as part of reality the worth of a poor person, a human embryo, a person with disabilities . . . it becomes difficult to hear the cry of nature itself. . . . Once the human being declares independence from reality and behaves with absolute dominion, the very foundations of our life begin to crumble. (116)

If rugged individualism sees salvation as exclusive to the individual, then the throwaway culture viciously extends this individualism to everyone and everything. The homeless man on the street has nothing to contribute to society so we can pass him by without a second thought. The unborn infant in the womb can be aborted because it's really the lives of the strong that matter. The person with disabilities is expendable because he or she is not capable of dwelling "normally" in society. The undocumented immigrant can be treated as garbage by customs agents, because he or she is "not one of us."

The throwaway culture, as described by Pope Francis, is not just a matter of human beings being bad people. It's a culture, a series of unexamined assumptions that do not allow us to see the humanity of others. Men and women are not distinct persons whom I encounter. Instead, they are "objects" for me to use (or not to use) depending on my needs. Every relationship is expendable.

The throwaway culture is a problem of commitment, of the impermanence of everything. This impermanence to all relationships can be a significant challenge for those seeking to attend a weekly celebration of the Eucharist that is, for the most part, the same from week to week. The throwaway culture problematizes establishing relationships in parishes in which we move beyond isolated monads who go to the same church toward living in solidarity as brothers and sisters in Christ. Many attending our parishes will find Mass to be a significant source of inspiration *until* they don't. And at that point, they may move on to something that better meets their needs. Rather than see themselves as part of a pilgrim band of brothers and sisters, moving toward Christ, they may painfully recognize the hypocrisy of other believers—determining that it'd be easier to go it alone in life than deal with this group of sinners.

The "Liturgy" of Consumerism

If there is a practice that is especially formative of human beings in a throwaway culture, it's shopping in a consumer society. Often, we think about consumerism as a matter of acquisition. The more stuff we have, the happier we will be. Certainly, this assumption exists among many people. Americans have so much stuff that we've invented a business whereby we pay money to put things that won't fit into our house elsewhere—storage warehouses.

But it's too simplistic to argue that consumerism is about only stuff. For example, I have an addiction to buying books. It is rare for me to finish an academic tome without purchasing one or two additional books online that were mentioned in footnotes. On my honeymoon, I dragged my poor wife to a seedy neighborhood in London so that I could spend four hours perusing a theological bookshop. I love books.

What is the source of this love? It's not just an addiction to being in the presence of lots of books. Otherwise, libraries could fulfill my addiction with greater ease. At Notre Dame, I have millions of books that I can check out, making it possible for me to dwell in the presence of thousands of serious and ancient tomes at once.

No, I love books because, in purchasing books, I get a kick. I see a book that I want. I search for it online. I find it. Then, I buy the book, eagerly awaiting its arrival at my door. I open the package, exhilarated to be in the presence of a new tome. After scanning the book, I place it on a shelf and feel, momentarily, the august accomplishment of being an academic—someone who is the kind of person who reads books like this.

The "liturgy" of consumerism for me is about shaping a certain kind of self through the act of acquisition. I want to be seen as an academic, as someone who pursues wisdom through reading and writing. Of course, anyone can (and does) buy books. One doesn't need a degree to do so. But somehow, the acquisition of books has become for me a way of expressing my identity as an academic. I don't need to read or even know what is in the book. Simply having the book on a shelf shows everyone who comes into my office, *this is a learned person.*

Consumer practice is thus shaping a certain kind of person through "practices" of shopping that are often unrelated to what it means to "become" this kind of person. Buying yoga pants doesn't turn one into a practitioner of yoga. Purchasing soccer cleats doesn't make one a World Cup star—otherwise, call me Ronaldo. To become this kind of person would require taking on a series of practices related to either yoga or soccer that would actually cultivate this self. Consumerism confuses the hard work of cultivating an identity with purchasing power. I buy, therefore I am.

Worship That Heals

As any doctor knows, there is often a bit of pain that takes place even in the midst of healing. The malaises that blossoming Christians and perhaps those of us who work in the RCIA suffer from can in fact be healed through commitment to liturgical practice. The act of liturgical worship may be hard for the modern person because of our belief in an absent God, a rugged individualism, a hope in technological salvation, a loss of wonder, a throwaway culture, and the "liturgy" of consumerism. But it is precisely our experience of worshiping in the church that can also heal us of these sicknesses. For in the liturgy we are taught to see the reality of God irrupting in history, to dwell together in communion, to expect salvation not from ourselves but from God, to wonder at beauty, to be committed to the dignity of the human person, and to experience the world as gift.

The language of healing has been intentionally chosen. During the precatechumenate, much of the work on the part of the catechist is one-on-one. A doctor doesn't show up with a program of health and walk away. A doctor listens to the needs of the patient and then offers a good medicine.

That's what we do as catechists. We enter into conversations with men and women about what really matters to them. Yet even here, there is a bit of teaching that's possible. It's not an education that unfolds in a classroom but the wisdom that is shared by intergenerational groups of parents who get together to talk about how to choose a good school for their kid.

I often engage in this kind of teaching during office hours. Students come to me not simply with problems they're having with material but with big questions about life: How do I know if I'm in love? How do I know what I'm called to do with my life? What does it mean to be a serious Catholic who also works in the world?

It would be naïve to simply say that each person has to find his or her own way. They've come to me because they see me as a "doctor," as someone who can provide a bit of wisdom on their pilgrimage. And I do. For the persons wondering if they're in love, I give examples from my own marriage and family life. But I also ask questions of them—how do they understand love, for example?

The medicine that we can offer many of our seekers will be from the liturgy. The rest of this section provides a handbook of sorts for those looking to heal some of the malaises of the contemporary person through reference to the church's worship. The hope is that readers will not just be happy with what is in the handbook but will adapt the examples and stories for their own use as catechists and spiritual mentors to those seeking to know something more about Christian faith.

The Irrupting God

Moralistic Therapeutic Deism is a malaise in which men and women cannot understand the presence of a God involved in human history. God is "out there," taking some notes, but mostly inattentive to creation. When such men and women encounter suffering in life, they can only assume that this God doesn't care or is without power.

The God that we worship in Catholic liturgy is not the deity adored by even these accidental Moralistic Therapeutic Deists. In the liturgy, we encounter a God who has entered history, forever transforming what it means to be human. On the feast of the Annunciation, when we commemorate the Blessed Virgin Mary's radical yes to God's plan of salvation, the church prays:

> O God, who willed that your Word
> should take on the reality of human flesh
> in the womb of the Virgin Mary,
> grant, we pray,
> that we, who confess our Redeemer to be God and man,
> may merit to become partakers even in his divine nature.
> Who lives and reigns with you in the unity of the Holy Spirit,
> one God, for ever and ever.
> (*Roman Missal*, The Annunciation of the Lord, Collect)

The Word became flesh in the womb of the Blessed Virgin. God becomes human. And this intimate union of God and humanity in the person of Jesus has global repercussions for us. The incarnation is not a "past" event but has infinite meaning for the present. We human beings can become partakers in the divine nature of Jesus Christ not through leaving behind our humanity. The more we enter into the human condition by giving our will over to God, just like the Blessed Virgin Mary, the more that we become divine.

The feast of the Annunciation is not unique in Catholic liturgy. Every celebration, every feast we commemorate focuses on a concrete way that God entered into history. But it also shows how God's involvement in history is the pattern for our present and future too. At Easter we remember that Jesus has risen from the dead, keenly hopeful that our death will be transformed in Christ. We will rise again, for God has defeated death. On the feast of All Souls, we commemorate the blessed dead themselves, knowing through faith that even the vale of tears caused by death cannot cut us off from communion with one another in Christ.

The liturgy teaches us that God has not abandoned the person who experiences suffering in his or her life. Instead, the limitations that are part of being human can now become the space where God irrupts in history. God is neither uninvolved nor powerless. Rather, God is present at the heart of our joys and sorrows alike, promising the possibility of redemption through the presence of Jesus Christ, the beloved Son. Talk about a provocation!

Made for Communion

Linked with Moralistic Therapeutic Deism is a rugged individualism, whereby we are trained to imagine that we are saved exclusively as individuals. Blossoming Christians, struggling with this assumption, may find it difficult to worship within the context of the ecclesial community. They'll be disappointed to discover that our liturgies are places not just for individual contemplation but for communion with Christ's Body. They may encounter the disappointment of scandal, of individual Christians who, although they identify as Catholics, are also public sinners.

The grammar of the church's liturgy can be salutary here. An astute catechist should underline the language of the church's prayers. The church does not use the first-person singular in the eucharistic prayer: I celebrate or commemorate. Instead, the church's eucharistic praying is a common activity, offered in the first-person plural: we celebrate or we remember. In the preface for the Eucharistic Prayer for Reconciliation I, the church prays:

> For you do not cease to spur us on
> to possess a more abundant life
> and, being rich in mercy,
> you constantly offer pardon
> and call on sinners
> to trust in your forgiveness alone.
>
> Never did you turn away from us,
> and, though time and again we have broken your covenant,
> you have bound the human family to yourself
> through Jesus your Son, our Redeemer,
> with a new bond of love so tight
> that it can never be undone. (*Roman Missal*)

Notice that the church does not plead before God that the individual alone would experience conversion. The entire church is called to ask for pardon, God never turns away from us, the whole family of God is invited to a confession of sins, and we join with the heavenly hosts to adore God. Even related to sinfulness, where we often focus on the individual alone, the church thinks about the entire body of believers. It is the church herself who is on pilgrimage to the Father, whose members are both burdened by sin and yet also redeemed through the graciousness of our Lord.

In the liturgy, we discover that we are made for communion, for friendship with one another in Christ. The liturgy teaches this not only through the texts of the prayer. Several years ago, I attended a Benedictine monastery where we were chanting Evening Prayer together. Entering the assembly, I sang the opening hymn with full gusto. An older Benedictine monk pulled me aside during the prayer, asking me to quiet down so that I could listen to the person on my left and right. My first reaction was annoyance. How dare he tell me how to express praise to the living God! But on deeper reflection, I realized there was a deep wisdom to this

Benedictine practice. The individual's prayer is not his or her own. It is always a single voice of praise offered to the Father through the Son within the context of the church. Since then, I enter into the church's worship aware of those around me, conforming my own responses to the person to my left and right. I seek to allow my voice to join with theirs.

This small practice has transformed how I engage in the liturgy. I am not a single individual, catering to my own personal salvation. I am involved in a common act with my neighboring parishioner whether we know each other well or not. As I join my voice with theirs, I've learned concern for every dimension of their lives. I've learned to recognize that I'm involved in the salvation of my children, my spouse, and my neighbors. We are made for communion.

Salvation through God Alone

A mark of modernity is an expectation that technology can save us. If we create the right medicine, develop the proper technological device, or create a suitable source of renewable energy, we can live forever. We *could* save ourselves.

In the church's worship, there is a univocal focus on the source of all salvation—the redemption of the world through Jesus Christ. Even our individual good works are possible through Christ alone. On the Third Sunday in Ordinary Time, we pray:

> Almighty ever-living God,
> direct our actions according to your good pleasure,
> that in the name of your beloved Son
> we may abound in good works. (*Roman Missal*, Collect)

Human activity, no matter how well intentioned, cannot save. Rather, every good deed is possible only because every dimension of our lives must be oriented to Christ. God has intervened in history. And now, God acts in history to bring men and women to salvation through the church.

This logic is found everywhere in the church's prayer. Yes, people need to come to Mass. Yes, they need to give themselves over to the sacramental life of the church. Yes, we must offer our humanity as the place where God will act. But this salvation does not unfold because people cared enough to pray. It is not because there is a community of really nice men and women who belong to a parish. Salvation happens because God has acted in history. Because in the eucharistic liturgy of the church, it's not we who lift ourselves up to God but heaven that comes to dwell among us as we join our voices with the divine praise of the city of God: "And so, with Angels and Archangels, with Thrones and Dominions, and with all the hosts and Powers of heaven, we sing the hymn of your glory, as without end we acclaim" (*Roman Missal*, Preface I of Advent).

Reverence in the liturgy demonstrates the salvific seriousness of worship. Such reverence need not be stuffy. Over the years, I've often attended daily Mass at Westminster Cathedral in London. In the parish, there is a boys' choir who processes in at the beginning of Mass, dressed in choral surplice. They're obviously boys, struggling to keep a straight face. They're awkward, and they sometimes trip a bit while turning to the left or right. But there is seriousness about their act of worship that exhibits to the assembly that something rather important is happening at the cathedral. God comes to dwell among us through the joyful seriousness of these well-trained, musical children.

Even the simplest gestures at Mass can manifest the seriousness of our act of worship. An acolyte who genuflects before the altar of God when lighting a candle establishes a reverence within a space that can transform even the emptiest of churches. Incense creates an atmosphere that reveals that a church building is different from a school or mall. The elevated language of a collect or eucharistic prayer says that something different is happening here—something salvific.

When we celebrate the Eucharist or the Liturgy of the Hours we make available to the world the firstfruits of God's reign. Men and women come forth, offering their wounded hearts to the triune God who promises that all tears will be wiped away. In the

Eucharist, especially, Christ comes entirely to dwell among us, pitching his tent in our midst. In order to avoid communicating a sense that it's really our work that saves, the church has to get out of the way in the liturgy, allowing God to act in the midst of Christ's Body.

The Wonder of Beauty

The loss of wonder, as described above, is a twofold concern. We cease to wonder, to attend to the glorious nature of reality because we're too focused on our smartphones to pay attention to the world. Staring at Facebook or Instagram, we no longer look down at our playing children. Likewise, the loss of this wonder risks eliminating spaces for meditation in our lives. We need quiet places where we can encounter that which is most beautiful, good, and true—in the process, asking ourselves what such beauty, goodness, and truth means for the rest of our lives.

Beauty has an important role to play in restoring wonder to the human condition. As mentioned above, I'm a hiker. And on a regular basis, I find myself taking long treks to out-of-the-way mountains with vistas that take one's breath away. Some years ago, I took high school students from Newton, Massachusetts, on a hike in a Pennsylvania state park. The hike was no more than half a mile, but these city dwellers had never been on such a trail. As we climbed up the short trail to a tower overlooking the mountains, they were struck with awe. They said that they had never seen anything so beautiful as these mountains. Along the hike, they began to have the kind of serious conversations about their future that I had always hoped would take place in the context of the youth group. Being around beauty opened them to deep conversations about things that matter.

I've also seen this happen with my graduate students that I teach in a summer course on liturgical-sacramental catechesis. I hold the first two hours of class at the Basilica of the Sacred Heart on Notre Dame's campus. A church building filled with gold, stained glass, statues, gorgeously decorated columns, and a variety of altars is to function as their "contemplative" space for 120 minutes. Their assignment in class that day is to spend time looking at things. In encountering such beauty, I encourage them to draw, write poetry, and journal as a way of creating a space for wonder. Univocally, they tell me from year to year that this was their favorite class day not only because I didn't lecture but because they were given a space to wonder, to contemplate the gift of divine love, in a purposeless manner.

One would imagine that our liturgies could provide a space of wonder in the present world. But often, silent wonder is absent from our celebrations. Priests are quick to say too much in their preaching or in opening remarks at the beginning of Mass. The prayers of the Mass are not chanted but are clumsily spoken aloud.

Liturgical music, so important to our sense of beauty, is often viewed, as a Jesuit colleague of mine says, as "sprinkles on top." What really matters at Mass are the words that are spoken. Music, architecture, incense, and statuary are optional accessories to the real meat of the liturgy—speech.

If we want to create a space of wonder in the lives of those coming to Mass, beauty matters. We have perhaps allowed a certain rationalism to enter into our worship, one where our focus is on endless chattering. As then-Cardinal Joseph Ratzinger cautions:

> Being struck and overcome by the beauty of Christ is a more real, more profound knowledge than mere rational deduction. Of course we must not underrate the importance of theological reflection, of exact and precise theological thought; it remains absolutely necessary. But to move from here to disdain or to reject the impact produced by the response of the heart in the encounter with beauty as a true form of knowledge would impoverish us and dry up our faith and our theology. We must rediscover this form of knowledge; it is a pressing need of our time. (Message of His Eminence Cardinal Joseph Ratzinger to the Communion and Liberation Meeting at Remini)

The example that I always use when speaking about beauty in worship is incense. Many parishes use incense once or twice a year at Christmas or Easter. This sparse use of incense misses an occasion for all our senses to participate in God's beauty. Our eyes are drawn to the way that light enters the church, refracted through the smoky haze. The smell of incense becomes part of old churches, serving as an embodied memory of the sacred rituals performed within the walls of the church. Even the sound of the thurible clinking becomes part of the beauty of the eucharistic encounter with Christ. In Catholicism, matter matters.

When we delight the senses in worship, we are facilitating an encounter with Jesus Christ and the worshiper. I'll always remember the Easter Triduum weekend that changed my life. I was a freshman at Notre Dame, where I was also an undergraduate seminarian with the Congregation of Holy Cross. But I was lost. I wanted God to be direct, to tell me my future. Was I to be a priest or not?

These questions came with me as I wandered into the half-lit basilica at eleven o'clock at night for Tenebrae. The air still smelled of the incense that had accompanied the Blessed Sacrament to the chapel of repose for the evening. I crowded into a pew, surrounded by other Notre Dame undergraduates, faculty, and staff. Over the next hour, I was moved by an encounter with the beauty of the liturgy. I remember the haunting voice of the cantor: *Jerusalem, Jerusalem, return to the Lord your God.* The choir sang a setting of the *Kyrie* composed by Louis Vierne from his *Messe solennelle,* Op. 16. This piece culminates in a crescendo in which the entire body of the listener is seemingly filled with sound. My very chest felt like it was going to explode, crying out with all my being for God's gracious mercy. All the while, seminarians from Holy Cross extinguished candles that were at the front of the altar. In the passion of Christ, we were entering into the darkness. At the end, the church was pitch black as the assembly participated in the *strepitus,* banging on the pews with their hands. It was loud, appropriate for a liturgical action meant to symbolize the earthquake after Christ's death.

The liturgy ended, and we processed out after midnight. My senses had been filled with beauty during the hour and a half liturgy. I wandered down to the Grotto at Notre Dame, a replica of the one in Lourdes, France, where the Blessed Virgin Mary appeared to St. Bernadette. I knelt in prayer, asking God once more to reveal my future. And in response to this prayer, a passage from the psalms came to my mind, "The LORD is my light and my salvation" (Ps 27:1).

On this cool spring night, I spent time meditating on this phrase surrounded by glowing candles at the Grotto. Over the next hour, still swimming in the beauty of the liturgy, I realized something. God had no plans to "tell me" the future. Instead, God is that light which illumines our steps. Christ is there with us in the darkness, asking us to give our wills over to the Father. It was not a matter of figuring out my future. Instead, I had to learn to sit in patient love even in the darkness of the unknown.

Surely, someone could have told me this directly. In fact, I have no doubt that someone did. My rector in seminary probably sat down and said to me during one of our one-on-one sessions, "Tim, you have the wrong understanding of God. God isn't an old man in heaven, leaving irritating clues for you to figure out your future." But it was only in the wondrous space created in the liturgy that I could finally see who God was. This was the God who never abandoned Israel, who died on the cross out of the depths of love, and who dwells now in the church. If I entered into this practice of self-giving love, then I would find God wherever I ended up. To have this insight on my own, I needed the wondrous beauty of the liturgy.

Beauty has this kind of power. And we want to include beauty in the liturgy not because we're a bunch of aesthetes who like pretty things. Beauty is part of how God communicates to us human beings. And it's how we, as human beings, find space to be alone with God.

The Liturgical Dignity of the Human Person

Recall the earlier discussion of the throwaway culture. The throwaway culture does not recognize the personhood of my neighbor, especially if he or she is on the margins. The unborn, the immigrant, and the prisoner can be treated without dignity because they're not of use to me.

The liturgy can provoke a worshiper to perceive the dignity in one's neighbor. Think, for example, about infant baptism. The infant, unable to make decisions on one's own, to speak, and even to control the bladder, enters into sacramental life. The nonspeaking, nonrational infant becomes a priest, a prophet, and a royal figure capable of sanctifying the created order even as a baby. All of those lowered in the waters of baptism, with no exception for race, socio-economic status, and education, are transformed into Christians. Every person in the church has this liturgical dignity, a vocation to adore the living God.

I think about this often as men and women process to Communion. In a downtown parish in Chicago, I see men and women with Down Syndrome, immigrants from throughout the world, and homeless men and women coming off the street. The dignity of each person is obvious to me in such moments. Every human being, no matter how rich or poor, educated or impoverished, has a vocation to adore the living God.

But it's not just people who are dignified in the liturgy. Through our celebration of liturgy, we discover there is nothing in creation that can merely be thrown away, treated only for its economic value. Everything in the world has a primary use, which is the glorification of God. One of my favorite prayers from the dedication of a church building perfectly expresses the liturgical vocation of creation:

> For you have made the whole world a temple of your glory,
> that your name might everywhere be extolled,
> yet you allow us to consecrate to you
> apt places for the divine mysteries.
>
> And so, we dedicate joyfully to your majesty
> this house of prayer, built by human labor.
> (*Roman Missal*, For the Dedication of a Church)

In this prayer, all of creation serves as a divine temple, pointing to God's glory on hilltop and plain alike. The church building is not a space apart from the rest of the world but instead attunes our eyes to see the world for what it is—infused with the spirit of divine love. The material construction of the church is itself a sign, pointing to the temple of Christ's Body and the heavenly Jerusalem. Our bodies are like temples, consecrated to God for the sanctification of the world. The stones of the church building are signs of each one of us, who make up a holy city whose constitution is eucharistic love.

The problem with a throwaway culture is that it's a form of idolatry, a failure to recognize that creation is gift. We are not made as isolated individuals who can dominate one another. We have been created for love. The liturgy reforms our imaginations to see this fact anew.

A Gift Economy

Consumerism is not just about purchasing things. It's about a misunderstanding of how identity formation takes place. I "become" a person through buying things.

But that's not how identity formation takes place. Becoming a Christian takes work. It's not a matter of buying a Bible or a copy of the Liturgy of the Hours or of updating one's Facebook page with regular posts from Bishop Robert Barron. In each of these "consumer" cases, the work of being a Christian is entirely up to me. It's a matter of exchange: I perform this action and thus become a Christian.

Many blossoming Christians, seeking entrance into the Christian life, may struggle with the gift economy of Christian life. They may see individual practices as something they "do" in order to "receive" grace. They buy; God gives. And they may be surprised that these practices take time. They take time because no human being can control divine generosity. The initial posture of the worshiping Christian is reception, not bargaining with God for grace.

Catholicism operates according to a different economy. If the liturgy of consumerism teaches, "I buy, therefore I am," the church's liturgy forms us to become what we receive. Christian life does not pertain first and foremost to the individual acquiring anything. Christian existence is first gift. It's a response to a love that is first given.

Liturgical prayer operates according to this kind of economy— we offer back to God what is first given. In Eucharistic Prayer III, for example, the church offers to the Father what has been given through Jesus Christ:

> Therefore, O Lord, as we celebrate the memorial
> of the saving Passion of your Son,
> his wondrous Resurrection
> and Ascension into heaven,
> and as we look forward to his second coming,
> we offer you in thanksgiving
> this holy and living sacrifice. (*Roman Missal*)

The sacrifice of Christ at the heart of all liturgical prayer is God's total and absolute gift of love. In the Eucharist, this love becomes present among us. And the church having received this love now offers it back to God. Part of this offering is the church reforming itself so that God may make of us an offering. Each and every Christian must become this love that is received. That is part of the return gift.

This return gift takes time. On a regular basis, I struggle to both receive God's love and to offer it in return. I enter into Mass distracted by looming book projects or family problems. I'm too busy accompanying my daughter on a seemingly eternal pilgrimage around the church building. At the end of Mass, I find myself too easily angered by my son or daughter. The slow driver in front of me annoys me. I avoid the homeless man or woman on the street because they make me uncomfortable. I still suffer the effects of sin.

The genius of Catholic liturgy is that we have to enter into this process of reception and gift regularly. We go to Mass each Sunday. We rise to praise God in the morning. We interrupt our work-a-day schedule for worship. We conclude our evening through confessing our sins to God. Christian identity is not bought. It's what we become through the regular practice of receiving divine love and then giving it away. It's a slow process, more like marinating a roast than microwaving a hotdog.

Liturgical Evangelization

Above, I have highlighted some of the ways that liturgical prayer can be provocative for the contemporary person. Based on your experience in the RCIA, you could probably add your own provocations to this list. The hope is that, through this exercise, you've been able to see how important liturgical practice is even to the period of evangelization *before* the catechumenate.

For this reason, it's important that some of this work of evangelization is carried out through liturgical celebration. The RCIA does not presume that dingy church basements with poor lighting are the ideal settings for Christian formation. Nor for that matter does the rite specify that the period of the precatechumenate happens only at the beginning of the academic year. A robust commitment to the RCIA presumes that men and women are entering into the period of evangelization throughout the liturgical year. Much of the work of preevangelization will happen in one-on-one conversations. But for those learning to desire an encounter with Jesus Christ, it is essential that we provide a space for such an encounter.

One way that a parish might create this regular space of encounter is through a monthly celebration of Vespers. On this night, no parish activity would take place except for an adapted version of Vespers. Children in religious education, the choir, the men's group, and all those in formation within the RCIA would attend this liturgy.

The celebration of Vespers would function as a "school" of evangelization. The chanting or singing of psalms, with periods of silence, would give space for contemplative wonder. Lengthier passages from the Scriptures could be chosen, appropriate to the liturgical feast of the day, allowing the parish to encounter the beauty of salvation history. Hymns from a variety of different styles could appeal to the affections, fostering an encounter with the beautiful God. Finally, there could be preaching in the context of this adapted Vespers, enabling seekers and mature Christians alike to contemplate how the baptized have lived out the kerygma of the church.

Creating regular liturgical space for encounter is essential for seekers. While the liturgy is evangelizing, the Mass is a complicated prayer. There's lots of kneeling, sitting, standing, and responding that make a visitor stick out like a sore thumb. This monthly Vespers might be precisely the occasion that would convince a visitor to take a second look at the church. And it would do so in a comfortable, hospitable way. After Vespers, the various parish groups could gather to talk to one another, building the kind of community that is important not simply for the RCIA but for a flourishing liturgical life.

A proposal like this is rather simple. But it may ruffle some feathers. It may require those in charge of religious education to rededicate one class per month to this prayer. It would necessitate a real sense of evangelization among parishioners, actively inviting friends and neighbors to come and see. But hard work like this would result in a culture of liturgical evangelization, a sense that the church's prayer is essential to inviting people into an encounter with Jesus.

Provoked Catechumens

Liturgy provokes the blossoming Christian to desire God, to offer one's whole life as a gift of love. The seeker, the one longing to meet Jesus Christ, begins to accept healing through the church's liturgy. It is thus appropriate that the church celebrates the acceptance of the candidate into the order of catechumens through a liturgical rite that repeats the healing they have already received.

Rite of Acceptance

The stage of the precatechumenate ends with the Rite of Acceptance into the Order of Catechumens. Enrollment into the catechumenate is not like transitioning from primary to secondary school. Rather, it's a change in the catechumens' identity. Catechumens are part of what the church calls an "order." The catechumen is now "ordered" toward initiation into the church. And catechumens have certain rights that come with their new identity—they may marry within the church using the appropriate rite and receive a Christian burial.

Entrance into the catechumenate should not be automatic. As the rite requires, "The prerequisite for making this first step is that the beginnings of the spiritual life and the fundamentals of Christian teaching have taken root in the candidates" (RCIA 42). The catechumen-to-be should show signs that he or she is involved in a life of prayer and understands and has some experience of belonging to the church.

The catechist should engage in a process of evaluation with each catechumen-to-be. This evaluation is not meant to be judgmental, whereby a priest or catechist makes an assessment as to whether someone is "worthy" to be a catechumen. Instead, the sponsors, catechists, deacons, and priests together "have the responsibility for judging the outward indications of such dispositions" (RCIA 43).

The category of provocation may be helpful in making such an assessment. The question could be asked, "Has the catechumen-to-be been provoked by his or her involvement in the life of the church?" Attending Mass, are they asking questions about the nature of a eucharistic life? Have they experienced the beginning fruits of conversion, worshiping the triune God rather than politics, prestige, or economic power? Do they have a sense that salvation is not the activity of an individual but deeper entrance into participation in the mystery of the church, in the friendship of believers? Whatever questions one asks, the process of inquiry should provoke the catechumen-to-be to articulate the way that his or her life has already been changed by an encounter with the mystery of Christ.

The Rite of Acceptance into the Order of Catechumens should take place within the community of the faithful. There is no single time of year that the rite should be celebrated. In fact, it could occur several times per year if there were a sufficient number of catechumens. The rite begins either at the entrance of the church or ideally outside. The location of the rite at the beginning is intentional. The catechumen-to-be, who is on the outside looking in, is about to enter into a new relationship with the church through acceptance into the order of catechumens.

Importantly, the priest or deacon goes to greet the catechumens-to-be. There is a wisdom to this liturgical action, one that should be transformative for the entire parish. A parish should not just wait for people to arrive at its door but should go out to invite men and women into the salvation available in Christ. The celebrant's first words upon greeting these catechumens-to-be should be one of welcome. This is a joyful occasion, a *celebratio* worth celebrating. At this point, the sponsors and candidates are invited to come forward, still outside the church or at the entrance of the parish, accompanied by singing. The rite recommends Psalm 63:1-8, which reads:

> O God, you are my God—
>> it is you I seek!
> For you my body yearns;
>> for you my soul thirsts,
> In a land parched, lifeless,
>> and without water.
> I look to you in the sanctuary
>> to see your power and glory.
> For your love is better than life;
>> my lips shall ever praise you!
> I will bless you as long as I live;
>> I will lift up my hands, calling on your name.
> My soul shall be sated as with choice food,
>> with joyous lips my mouth shall praise you! (Ps 63:1-6)

Psalm 63 is provocative! It uses language like thirst, faint, seek, and behold. The catechumens-to-be who listen to this psalm and the assembly gathered in worship come to recognize that Christian salvation is about desire. This rite is not just a quaint exercise for recruiting new members to the church. Likewise, the psalm provokes by promising what will come at the end of initiation. There will be water to quench the thirsty soul. There will be a feast of Christ's Body and Blood. How can those of us who have been baptized into Christ, who celebrate the Eucharist from week-to-week, not be provoked ourselves as we recognize the wondrous gift of Christian life celebrated in the liturgy!

The rite continues with an opening dialogue. The celebrant asks the candidates to state their names. They are also asked to express their desire for faith and eternal life with God. Although the rite allows for a large group of candidates to be asked these questions as a group, it is appropriate, if the group is small enough, to ask each individual. Each individual person comes to the church with his or her story. And his or her "I" is to become part of the church's "We." My desire for faith, my longing for eternal life with God is to be shared in this community of faith.

After the dialogue, each candidate (if the group is small enough) is asked to express his or her acceptance of the Gospel. The candidate hears a shortened proclamation of the kerygma. This moment of the rite follows the pattern of liturgical remembering that heals us from Moralistic Therapeutic Deism. Eternal life is not entering some out-of-the-way place we call heaven. It is knowledge of Jesus Christ who has entered into history, who has died and risen from the dead, and who is ruler of the created order. Salvation involves making every part of our identity conform to the self-giving love of Jesus Christ, letting salvation history become our history. To accept the Gospel is not to accept a series of abstract precepts delivered from on high. It is instead to give oneself over to a new story, a new history revealed in Christ. The candidates' acceptance of the kerygma is more than a general agreement with what the priest or deacon has said. It's a commitment of the self, the most important liturgical offering that the candidate has made thus far.

This commitment is not exclusively an individual one. Having committed to life with Christ, the church through the ministry of the sponsor pledges fidelity to the candidate. The sponsor and the entire assembly promise to "help these candidates find and follow Christ" (RCIA 53). The church pledges to live out the eucharistic life at the heart of her identity—to become a place where divine love dwells. The homily during the Liturgy of the Word should underline not only the commitment of the new catechumen but the loving obligation to shepherd these fledgling Christians to participate in the mystery of salvation.

The Rite of Acceptance into the Order of Catechumens is not exclusively verbal. The rite includes a signing of the forehead by the celebrant, as well as optional rites of signing each of the senses by the catechists or sponsors. An action, such as signing each of the senses, is a ritual performance that effects the transformation taking place in the soon-to-be-catechumen. The celebrant declares:

> N., receive the cross on your forehead.
> It is Christ himself who now strengthens you
> with this sign of his love.
> Learn to know him and follow him. (RCIA 55A)

The transformation that the new catechumen has undergone is not the result of his or her serious study, the sponsor's charism, or the presider's good preaching. It is Jesus Christ who is the primary actor who transforms the candidate into a catechumen, into one who seeks total union with Christ. Such a transformation involves the entirety of one's body. The ears are signed so that one may hear the voice of God. The candidate-become-catechumen receives the sign of the cross on the eyes so that he or she may perceive God's glory in every dimension of creation. The lips are signed so that the catechumen can respond in praise to God's glory. The breast is signed so that Christ may dwell in the heart of the catechumen. The shoulders are signed so that the catechumen may bear the gentle yoke of Christ to the world. And then each catechumen is blessed by the presider, a blessing that recognizes the wondrous transformation that has taken place.

Imagine an assembly, still gathered outside the church, watching this transformation. What would it provoke to a Catholic who has become bored with the church? To young children, baptized in infancy, coming to recognize what it means to belong to Christ's

Body? Catholicism isn't just a nice tradition. It's an entrance into salvation that takes up every dimension of our humanity.

The celebrant then offers a concluding prayer. Only now do the catechumens and the sponsors come forward into the church, preparing to hear the Liturgy of the Word. The rite suggests that they come forward, singing selected verses from Psalm 34 in which the soul cries out for divine wisdom. This psalm provides a lens for understanding the liturgical nature of the catechumens' vocation. Having enrolled in the catechumenate, the catechumens and assembly together participate in the Liturgy of the Word. After the readings and homily, intercessions are offered on behalf of the catechumens. They will now be prayed over and dismissed before the Liturgy of the Eucharist. Even if they have attended Mass for years with their families, as is often the case, they may no longer stay for the Liturgy of the Eucharist. This isn't because the church does not want to feed them with the finest of foods. The catechumen is learning to eat, to chew on the wisdom of God found in the Scriptures. The catechumenate is a time to hunger for the Word of God, to seek the Lord alone. The homily should have touched on these themes. Likewise, it is appropriate that a Bible be given to the catechumen at this point, for the liturgical object *par excellence* for the catechumen is the Scriptures.

As already mentioned, this moment of dismissal could be misinterpreted. The catechumen could understand this moment as a separation from the communion of believers: Now that I'm a part of you, how could you ask me to leave? This isn't the right way to think about the dismissal. To be dismissed from the Eucharist is intended to increase desire. Originally, the dismissal during the catechumenate was intended to guard the mystery of the Eucharist. In the ancient world, one could not attend the eucharistic liturgy except if one was baptized. For us, people attend Mass all the time who are not part of the communion of the church. We don't throw them out.

So when we dismiss the catechumens the intention is to provoke deep desire for the Eucharist. The longing for the Eucharist does not begin right before the Easter Vigil. It is a hunger that is to take over every dimension of the catechumen's being. And likewise, the catechumen serves a liturgical function for each member of the baptized assembly. It is easy for us baptized Christians to forget the wondrous nature of our vocation. We grow complacent with showing up. But each time a catechumen is dismissed from our midst, we should wonder anew about the glorious gift of the Eucharist that we receive weekly or even daily.

Conclusion

Liturgical prayer is provocative. Liturgy provokes not through violent rhetoric or salacious content. It provokes because the liturgy provides a vision of human happiness that inevitably butts up against other ways of living. For seekers, regular participation in the liturgy can and should provide the best introduction to the gift of love at the heart of Christian life. And good catechists will lead these seekers to understand how the logic of love at the heart of liturgical prayer may be calling them to a new way of life. The Rite of Acceptance into the Order of Catechumens fully reveals the power of Christian liturgy in transforming men and women into disciples of Jesus Christ.

Those provoked by the liturgy will hopefully want to enter more deeply into Christian formation. They'll move from being seekers to entering into the order of catechumens. And here, the church through the worshipful wisdom of the catechist will be able to propose the hypothesis that answers the question at the heart of being a human being: we are made for worship.

Chapter 2

Liturgical Formation in the Catechumenate

It was late March in South Bend and still very cold. After a semester of studying the Old and New Testaments, we were about to read Augustine's *Confessions*. It was a book that I had wanted to examine for years, and at last the time had come. Looking around the room at weary faces, I suspected that I was more excited about this opportunity than many of my classmates. The professor asked us to open the text of the *Confessions* to the very first paragraph. He joined us in the ritual opening of the text, reading along in his own well-marked copy. The professor began, "Great are you, O Lord, and exceedingly worthy of praise . . . " He stopped and turned to the chalkboard. In Latin, he wrote, *Magnus es Domine et laudabilis valde.*

"Do you know what this means?" he asked. Some of us, schooled in Latin, translated it, "Great are you, Lord, and exceedingly praiseworthy," we answered. "Good. But do you know what it means?" Over the next hour, the professor began to unfold what it means for a human being to cry out in praise to God. Human beings are creatures. We were made by God. And therefore, praise is integral to the human vocation. The Christian life has as its goal a restoration of the human person to this original worshipful vocation. For, as St. Augustine himself says, "Our heart is restless until it rests in you."

For the first time that semester, as a theology nerd surrounded by far cooler classmates, I knew that I was not alone in connecting with the material. My fellow undergraduates were aware of the restlessness of the human condition. They knew the paralyzing fear of wondering what was in store for our future. They understood the loneliness that nearly all freshmen experience as they long for friends and family at home. Whether they talked about it or not, they were acquainted with the daily question, "Who am I to become?" In reading Augustine, each of us found a potential answer to this question that we had never considered: We are made for worship, to adore the living God—nothing else could complete us.

This professor had offered us, unbeknownst to our still-adolescent selves, an ultimate hypothesis. It was the kind of proposal that necessitated each student examine the veracity of the claim. Do I think that the meaning of life is worship? Do I engage in the activity of study in a worshipful manner? If I lived a worshipful existence, if I made my whole life into a hymn of praise to the living God, what would happen? Is Augustine, in the end, right?

The Hypothesis of the Catechumenate

The period of the catechumenate is the period in which the church systematically proposes a total hypothesis based in Christian teaching to the catechumen. As the RCIA says, "This catechesis leads the catechumens not only to an appropriate acquaintance with dogmas and precepts but also to a profound sense of the mystery of salvation in which they desire to participate" (RCIA 75.1). The catechumenate links knowledge of the church's teaching with a desire to participate in the mystery of salvation that this teaching signifies.

The catechumenate provides beginners in faith with the rudiments of Christian teaching as an ultimate hypothesis. Here, the *Catechism of the Catholic Church* (CCC) is an essential resource. Too often this text functions as nothing more than an encyclopedia of church teaching. Careful readers of the text know that the *Catechism* proposes to the Christian the meaning of life, the way of seeking happiness. The *Catechism* hypothesizes that human happiness must be oriented to right praise, adoring the living God.

One can see this pedagogy of worshipful love throughout the *Catechism*. Quoting the catechism of the Council of Trent:

> The whole concern of doctrine and its teaching must be directed to the love that never ends. Whether something is proposed for belief, for hope or for action, the love of our Lord must always be made accessible, so that anyone can see that all the works of perfect Christian virtue spring from love and have no other objective than to arrive at love. (CCC 25)

Teaching Christian doctrine is not about mastering truth, becoming a super-Catholic by memorizing the *Catechism*. The *Catechism* proposes a hypothesis grounded in love. God has made the world in love. And we are made to offer back to God a return gift of love. The pedagogy of the *Catechism* facilitates this transformation.

In a fallen world, the *Catechism*'s ultimate hypothesis requires a bit of attention, for it is not evident to many human beings that the world has been created for love. Think about Fifth Avenue in New York City. If one invited some hypothetical space alien to wander down Fifth Avenue during Christmas, this space creature might come to a very different conclusion about the nature of human life. Human beings, according to this creature, are made for consumption. They sell products. They are made for glitz and glamour, perfume and lingerie, fame and fortune.

Each of us enters into the world as a kind of alien. We're not born into a world where the meaning of life is immediately evident. Someone has to tell us something about life, and they do. Fifth Avenue in New York City proposes something about the meaning of human life. But so does the *Catechism*. Human beings are made for worship: "The desire for God is written in the human heart, because man is created by God and for God; and God never ceases to draw man to himself" (CCC 27). Human beings, no matter how sinful, cannot irrevocably sacrifice their liturgical vocation. We are made to adore the living God, to give ourselves over to the triune God as a sacrifice of praise.

Christian doctrine is thus an apologetics of love whereby we learn what it means to be created for praise. Yes, if we are careful thinkers, attentive to the world, it's possible to discover the wondrous nature of creation itself. Who hasn't had their breath taken away by a sunset over a beach? Through cuddling with a newborn baby? But God has so loved humanity that God also reveals something about what it means to be God and human through divine revelation. As the *Catechism* argues:

> God who "dwells in unapproachable light" wants to communicate his own divine life to the men he freely created, in order to adopt them as his sons in his only-begotten Son. By revealing himself God wishes to make them capable of responding to him, and of knowing him, and of loving him far beyond their own natural capacity. (CCC 52)

God has entered into history through creation, the covenant with Israel, and redemption in Jesus Christ. Doctrine reveals to human beings the precise nature of a God who is total and absolute love and who longs for human beings to share in this divine life. Being a creature is wonderful. Yet God wants to give human beings something more. God wants us to become divine.

Catechesis during the catechumenate is that systematic process that facilitates entrance into the divine life through the communication of the ultimate hypothesis: God is love. Importantly, the church presumes that the period of the catechumenate lasts a sufficient period of time, even several years, so that the catechumens may themselves become a site of love (RCIA 76). The length of the catechumenate is not dependent on the liturgical calendar, the school year, or the quantity of material to be covered. Rather, conversion of mind, heart, and will alone matter. Instruction in this period should be "of a kind that while presenting Catholic teaching in its entirety also enlightens faith, directs the heart toward God, fosters participation in the liturgy, inspires apostolic activity, and nurtures a life completely in accord with the spirit of Christ" (RCIA 78). The "curriculum" for the RCIA is nothing short of what one needs to know to flourish in Christian living—how to offer one's whole being as a sacrifice of praise to the living God.

Liturgical formation is vital to each moment of teaching doctrine within the catechumenate. The church's *General Directory for Catechesis* describes liturgical formation in this way:

> The Church ardently desires that all the Christian faithful be brought to that full, conscious, and active participation which is required by the very nature of the liturgy and the dignity of the baptismal priesthood. For this reason, catechesis, along with promoting a knowledge of the meaning of the liturgy and the sacraments, must also educate the disciples of Jesus Christ "for prayer, for thanksgiving, for repentance, for praying with confidence, for community spirit, for understanding correctly the meaning of the creeds . . . ", as all of this is necessary for a true liturgical life. (GDC 85)

The end of liturgical formation is living the liturgy. The Christian well-disposed to living liturgically is the one who knows how to pray, who grasps that Christian doctrine is not equivalent to the philosophical teaching of Immanuel Kant. Instead, "knowledge" within Catholicism is intimately related to prayer (GDC 87).

The catechumenate presumes the formation of the Christian into a worshipful wisdom—knowing about the triune God also means adoring this God with the fullness of our being. While the remainder of this chapter will show how this formation unfolds through attention to specific liturgical and sacramental doctrine, it is important to remember that every church teaching has a liturgical orientation. Teaching knowledge of the faith or the moral life is linked to the liturgy. Let me give two examples: the church's teaching on the immaculate conception of the Blessed Virgin Mary and the virtue of solidarity.

The immaculate conception is a misunderstood doctrine among Catholics and those entering the church. The feast of the Immaculate Conception, celebrated on December 8, is not a commemoration of the conception of Jesus, as it is popularly understood, but of his mother, Mary. The doctrine expresses the conviction that Mary was born without sin. Jesus's mother-to-be received a gift from God, what the church calls "grace," before she was even born.

But why was Mary given this gift? The *Catechism* presents this mystery to us for contemplation:

> At the announcement that she would give birth to "the Son of the Most High" without knowing man, by the power of the Holy Spirit, Mary responded with the obedience of faith, certain that "with God nothing will be impossible": "Behold, I am the handmaid of the Lord; let it be [done] to me according to your word." Thus, giving her consent to God's word, Mary becomes the mother of Jesus. Espousing the divine will for salvation wholeheartedly, without a single sin to restrain her, she gave herself entirely to the person and to the work of her Son; she did so in order to serve the mystery of redemption with him and dependent on him, by God's grace. (CCC 494)

Being born without sin was not some special genius bestowed on the Blessed Virgin Mary for her own sake. She received this prevenient grace so that she could offer a truly free yes to God. In her yes, as the *Catechism* clarifies, Mary speaks for all of Israel and the church. For each of us, reborn into Christ, we are made to offer to God a total and absolute yes. And the Blessed Virgin Mary, who has received grace beyond grace, is an icon of what we are called to become—those who say to God, "Let it be done unto me . . . "

The doctrine of the immaculate conception is about the worship that each of us is called to practice. We human beings are made to give our full selves away in love. Through sin, we are sometimes reluctant to do so. God can have my intellect, I say to myself, but not my desire. God can be present with me on a Sunday during

Mass but not when I encounter homeless men and women in urban centers. God doesn't want this partial gift. God wants everything. And the Blessed Virgin Mary provides for us the horizon of what we can become if we learn to love her Son—we become those who give their full selves away in love.

Like the doctrine of the immaculate conception, the church's teaching relative to solidarity is often misunderstood. Folks can confuse solidarity with a vague feeling of sorrow at the suffering of our neighbor—"I feel you, bro." Or solidarity may be understood as a purely secular virtue, something that binds Christian and non-Christian together even if they can't agree on the identity of Jesus Christ as the savior of the world. If I believe in solidarity, then I don't need to think about the Trinity or the Eucharist.

Solidarity is more than a feeling or the foundation of a secular Christianity. Rather, it's a virtue linked to the dignity of the human person. Human beings are not objects for us to use. Human beings are persons, and thus they have rights that are prior to how a society defines what it means to be a human being. And each person, no matter what society he or she belongs to, is my neighbor insofar as he or she is human like me. As the *Catechism* reports:

> Created in the image of the one God and equally endowed with rational souls, all men have the same nature and the same origin. Redeemed by the sacrifice of Christ, all are called to participate in the same divine beatitude: all therefore enjoy an equal dignity. (CCC 1934)

The destiny of each and every human being is adoration of the living God. The woman who suffers because her husband abuses her is my responsibility, for she is my neighbor. Solidarity is the cultivation of that virtue that enables me to share friendship with this woman, to see her plight as my own, and to do something to respond to her situation. A society is infused with solidarity when it no longer allows injustice to be inflicted on any person because this man and this woman are my neighbors. In reorienting itself to care for the neighbor, to end injustice, this society offers fruitful worship to the God who is love. Solidarity, even when it appears in the secular sphere, is already a Christian virtue.

The church's eucharistic liturgy gives us a proper sense of solidarity. The opening prayer for a Mass offered for charity reads:

> Set our hearts aflame, O Lord,
> with the Spirit of your charity, we pray,
> that we may always think thoughts
> worthy and pleasing to your majesty
> and love you sincerely in our brothers and sisters.
>
> (*Roman Missal*, For Charity, Collect)

Those of us aflame with divine charity, having encountered the God who is love, are not to keep this love for ourselves. Through the outpouring of the Spirit in the sacramental life, we are to reorient every dimension of our lives to love. God sustains us with divine blessing through our worship that we may share that divine blessing with others. And that means that our worship does not conclude with thinking pleasant thoughts about God. We must sincerely love our neighbor through taking up the virtue of solidarity, a continuation of the act of worship.

Thus, church doctrine is never reducible to abstract propositions that a believer can theoretically assent to. Rather, doctrine proposes to human beings who God is and what this means for human life. God is love, and human beings are made to offer the return gift of love—the whole self. During the catechumenate, every doctrine should be taught as pointing toward the worshipful wisdom and divine blessing that saves not only the individual person but also the whole world.

The Environment Proposes

A good catechist, one with a sufficient theological education, will be able to show how each doctrine relates to the adoration of the living God. But education is not reducible to the words we employ as catechists and sponsors. Instead, the environment in which we teach is part and parcel of the educative act.

The environment most used throughout the catechumenate is unfortunately the classroom. Over the last fifteen years, I have volunteered with six different catechumenate processes. Universally, the catechumens met in a space that resembled a classroom of some type. Sometimes, the space was a dingy church basement with an old chalkboard. Updated church basements might have a marker board! At other times, it was an august seminar room with a sturdy table. Sometimes, we'd leave these rooms to pray in the church or head out to the local Catholic Worker House to spend time with those on the margins in our community. But roughly 80 percent of the catechumens' formation unfolded in a classroom.

Now, let me be clear. Classrooms are important spaces in the lives of many men and women. As a professor of theology, I acknowledge that the classroom can be a sacred space where young students encounter ideas that can change their lives. But the purpose of the RCIA is not equivalent to the kind of theological education that a university gives. In the catechumenate, we are meant to learn to adore the living God, and for this reason, our education itself should be conducted in a worshipful milieu.

The grammar of the RCIA demands the presence of liturgical space as integral to the formation of catechumens. The rite clarifies:

> During the period of the catechumenate there should be celebrations of the word of God that accord with the liturgical season and that contribute to the instruction of the catechumens and the needs of the community. These celebrations of the word are: first, celebrations held specially for the catechumens; second, participation in the liturgy of the word at the Sunday Mass; third, celebrations held in connection with catechetical instruction. (RCIA 81)

Most parishes know that catechumens should participate in the Liturgy of the Word at Sunday Mass. A good number of these parishes, after dismissing the catechumens before the Liturgy of the Eucharist, engage in theological reflection around the Scriptures and other liturgical elements. But how many parishes locate catechetical instruction within the context of the Liturgy of the Word? How many include specific liturgies for the catechumens?

Locating catechetical instruction in the context of a celebration of the Word of God has implications for how one understands the act of catechesis. Catechesis for the RCIA is not "church jeopardy." Initiatory catechesis is an occasion to contemplate the wondrous love of the triune God, the ultimate hypothesis at the heart of Christian faith. Intellectual formation in the RCIA is oriented toward wisdom rather than mastery. It is concerned with beauty, with encounter, and with love.

Celebrations of the Word of God in the RCIA have the following parts. First, the liturgy begins with a hymn or song. Singing is important for learning to "remember" the Christian faith we are contemplating through formal study. The only way that I can still recall the quadratic formula is because my math teacher set it to music. Hymnody in the church has often served a similar function, forming the memory of Christians with the essential images that we need in order to adore the living God. I may not be able to recite the O Antiphons used before the *Magnificat* at Vespers from December 17 through December 24, but I do know "O Come, O Come Emmanuel."

Because of the importance of these images in Christian life, the catechist in the RCIA has a responsibility to assess the theological suitability of hymns. It is often argued that because hymns are poetic, they don't need to be precise. In some ways, this is true. We're not going to sing about the consubstantiality of the Father and the Son or the distinction between habitual and actual grace. But the hymns cannot be contrary to Christian doctrine. One can't sing a hymn that declares that creeds don't really matter, that human beings are responsible for their own salvation, or that the Eucharist is just really important bread and wine. These hymns might have great tunes, but they also are wrong. They form the memory of catechumens in imprecise or improper images.

Hymnody is not reducible to this pedagogical function of teaching the catechumen the proper images for understanding God. Hymns also assist us in recollecting specific moments of our lives, becoming part of our very encounter with God in history. The closing hymn for my wedding Mass was "O God Beyond All

Praising." Each time I sing this hymn at Sunday Mass or at some-one else's wedding, I don't just think about my wedding Mass. Instead, the hymn itself has become a living sign of the divine and human love I have experienced through nuptial love. The hymn has become the interpretative key for my marriage. Kara and I have learned to see every moment of our marriage as an occasion of blessing. And thus through this hymn, we have come to see the nuptial vocation as one of constant praise: "Whether our tomor-rows / be filled with good or ill, / we'll triumph through our sorrows / and rise to bless you still: / to marvel at your beauty / and glory in your ways, / and make a joyful duty / our sacrifice of praise." This hymn was a source of catechesis for us before we even knew what it would mean to be married in Christ. It was this musical phrase that carried us through the suffering we en-dured when diagnosed with infertility. The hymns we sing form catechumens in the Christian life, giving them words of praise and lament, that will sustain them through life.

After the hymn, the catechumens listen to readings from the Scriptures and respond through a psalm following each reading. Because the celebration of the Word of God is not part of a specific liturgical rite, any readings may be chosen. The readings may cor-respond to the liturgical year. Or they may be linked more closely to the doctrine or precept that will be treated through systematic catechetical instruction.

The activity of listening to the Scriptures and responding through a psalm has a pedagogical purpose. Hearing is an oc-casion of revelation. A sound occurs outside of the listener, re-verberating in the ear. Listening to the Word of God grounds all catechetical instruction in the moment of divine revelation. God first speaks. God acts. But God does not leave us paralyzed before the Word. We can respond, offering a word of praise in return.

The importance of the psalms, in particular, should be under-lined in such celebrations of the Word of God. The psalms are not ditties that make listening to the Bible more enjoyable. Instead, the psalms are part of the divine Scriptures, integral to the human history of responding to God's glory. We learn from the psalms that God does not simply want us to respond with praise. The Christian life of prayer, if it is to sustain us through the good and bad times alike, requires being honest with God. The psalms are often brutally honest with God. We cry out to God, asking why God isn't acting. We consecrate our anger against injustice through prayer. And we sit in glory before the God who has revealed the beauty of divine glory in creation.

Following the proclamation of the Scriptures and the psalmody, there is an occasion for a homily or moment of catechetical instruction. Note that the "catechesis" is located within a liturgical context. We don't just introduce the doctrine of the immaculate conception abstracted from the vocation of the human person to adore God. The doctrine is preached or taught within the context of prayer.

The homiletic quality to this catechetical instruction necessitates clear formation of the catechist in the art of preaching. In teaching a doctrine or precept, we're not just trying to clarify what the church means. We can't hand out a series of passages from the church's *Catechism*, asking if there are any questions. We're inviting the catechumen to participate in this doctrine. In the context of the feast of the Immaculate Conception, we must provoke from the catechumen the depth questions: What does it mean to be human? What do we long for? And we must show how this doctrine, as found in Scripture and Tradition, provides an answer to this question. The answer that we discover about the destiny of the human person in Jesus Christ, as evident in Mary his mother, does not close us off from seeking God. It instead leads us to long for God more. The moment of catechesis should be contemplative, prayerful, an invitation to encounter the mystery of love at the heart of the world.

Finally, the celebration of the Word of God ends with optional concluding rites. The catechumens may be given a minor exorcism. Some explanation is necessary here, lest one begin to conjure up an image of the film, *The Exorcist*.

First, the church does perform major exorcisms, the kind of sacramentals that most people think about when using the term "exorcism." Catholics believe that it's possible for a human being to be possessed by the devil. And, after assessing the possibility of a mental illness—which is not the same as demonic possession—a bishop or designated priest will perform a major exorcism. Major exorcisms aren't magic. Instead, as the *Catechism* clarifies, "Exorcism is directed at the expulsion of demons or to the liberation from demonic possession through the spiritual authority which Jesus entrusted to his Church" (CCC 1673). Through the power of the church, given by Jesus Christ, the church seeks to expel this demon from the life of an individual person.

The RCIA does not include major exorcisms. But the rite does have minor exorcisms. "Minor" here doesn't mean less important. These exorcisms "draw the attention of the catechumens to the real nature of Christian life, the struggle between flesh and spirit, the importance of self-denial for reaching the blessedness of God's kingdom, and the unending need for God's help" (RCIA 90). The exorcisms manifest to the catechumen, the sponsor, and catechists the seriousness of salvation. During the exorcism, the catechumen bows or kneels. The celebrant, who can be a priest, a deacon, or a designated catechist, prays with hands outstretched and offers a prayer over the catechumen. These prayers begin by recalling the gift of divine power, showing how Jesus Christ has acted to liberate men and women from sin and death. Likewise, these exorcisms pray that Jesus would act in the life of the catechumen right now. The prayer does not address an abstract evil in the life of the catechumen but invites the catechumen to an examination of conscience:

> Do not let their minds be troubled
> or their lives tied to earthly desires.
> Do not let them remain
> estranged from the hope of your promises
> or enslaved by a spirit of unbelief. (RCIA 94H)

The minor exorcisms end by asking for grace that the catechumen may unite him- or herself more closely to Christ and the entire church.

These exorcisms are formative not only of the catechumens, who learn to examine their lives for conformity to the mystery of love revealed in Christ, but for the priest, deacon, catechist, sponsor, and any member of the assembly who participates in these exorcisms. The Christian life is a pilgrimage toward holiness. We do not arrive when we are baptized, confirmed, and receive Christ's Body and Blood in the Eucharist. Ironically, those of us in the church for the longest period of time may be the ones who need these exorcisms the most. I can't help but think about the sexual abuse scandal that has been simmering in the church for the last fifty years. To me, ecclesial leadership would have benefited from regular opportunities to consider the effect of sinfulness in their lives, to recognize the various ways that the devil prowls like a roaring lion (cf. 1 Pet 5:8). The exorcisms underline that we Christians are never a finished product. Holiness is a horizon.

In addition to the exorcisms, the celebrations of the Word of God also include blessings. Like the exorcisms, the blessings demonstrate to the catechumen the salvific process that he or she is undergoing. These blessings also form the catechumens in the art of Christian prayer. Prayer always begins through calling out to God, remembering God's intimate involvement in human history. The blessing prayers ask God to act in our midst here and now, aware that Christian transformation is possible only through the power of the Spirit.

Between the exorcisms and the blessings, no catechumen can walk away from systematic catechesis thinking that Christian existence is something earned through intellectual or moral achievement. The Christian life is a gift, made possible through a divine generosity that precedes each of our desires. God acts to eliminate evil from our existence and then brings us into the gift of the church.

The RCIA also includes an Anointing of the Catechumens. Few parishes I have attended have included such regular anointings. This is a shame! Throughout Christian history, oil has been used to guard against the effects of evil. Oil is especially effective in this regard, reminding the catechumen of their unique status, insofar as oil involves multiple senses. One can smell the oil, feel its touch upon one's skin, see the oil on one's forehead. The Rite of Anointing begins with a prayer of exorcism and then continues to a blessing of the oil.

Likely, this anointing should not take place weekly. But the process of anointing once again allows the catechumen to recognize his or her unique status in the church. To anoint the catechumen with oil during this time shows how the body itself is part of this transformation. There is no place for abstract assent in the Christian life. The oil is given on the head, on both hands, and even other parts of the body. Becoming Christian involves our whole selves. The rest of the church, by participating in this anointing, recognizes the privileged vocation of the catechumens dwelling among us. These men and women are not just "future" Christians but are already sanctifying the created order here and now.

The rites belonging to the catechumenate ensure that initiatory catechesis is never understood within a purely scholastic framework. The RCIA is a school, but it is not a school concerned with academic formation exclusively. It is a school of Christian life whose mission is grounded in the appropriation of worshipful wisdom. Thus, the catechumenate is about creating an environment where the hypothesis of Christian faith can be slowly appropriated by the catechumen into a way of life.

The Liturgical-Sacramental Hypothesis

During the catechumenate, in addition to the celebration of the liturgy, it is appropriate to introduce the catechumen into the "grammar" of the church's sacramental system. It is important to provide liturgical experience, but it is also essential to give the catechumens the appropriate speech for describing their experience. Liturgical catechesis during the catechumenate should dispose the catechumen to participate fully, actively, and consciously in the liturgical life of the church. This education will involve two dimensions: competency and contemplation.

First, liturgical education during the catechumenate should begin with competency. Too often, Catholics who have belonged to the church for years forget the necessity of teaching basic liturgical postures. We learned such postures because we attended Mass as a child, discovering how to use our bodies in worship as we imitated our parents, the assembly, or our friends. We inherited our liturgical competency before we even recognized what we were doing.

My son, for example, has discovered how to participate in liturgies through worshiping with his parents. Without our example, he would have inevitably been lost, since no human creature is born knowing to sign one's head, lips, and heart when the gospel is read during Mass. Our son has learned from our example how to genuflect, how to sing the *Salve Regina* by heart during night prayer, and how to bow when the acolyte blesses the assembly with incense.

Catechumens need both the implicit example of sponsors and catechists as well as explicit instruction. Time should be set aside to walk the catechumens through the Mass, teaching them when, why, and how Catholics bow, genuflect, stand, cross themselves, and bless themselves with holy water. Key liturgical chants should also be taught. Over the course of the catechumenate, the Marian antiphons, the Lord's Prayer, the *Benedictus*, and the *Magnificat* should be taught. Sponsors have an important role here, since much of this teaching will best be accomplished through answering the questions of catechumens. Why does our parish do this? How do I genuflect? How do I pay attention during the homily when it's boring?

We forget this liturgical competency, I suspect, because we privilege knowledge about the liturgy and sacraments above capacity to participate in these sacraments. To form the body of the worshiper in the art of prayer should be the primary task of the catechumenate. Such bodily formation is part of learning to pray, part of being initiated into the Tradition of the church.

Nonetheless, since we're working with adults, we also need to provide more than bodily competency. As my son grows up, as he begins to ask questions, it is insufficient to exhort him to just kneel. He'll want to know why the church celebrates liturgy at all.

He'll want to know the rationale for the seven sacraments. He'll want to know something about the Liturgy of the Hours, why our family prays in the way that it does each evening. And when he asks questions about the way that he worships, he doesn't just want information. He wants a hypothesis—how is this action important to my destiny?

During the catechumenate, we owe the catechumens a hypothesis concerning the nature of liturgical prayer, the sacraments, the liturgical year, and the Liturgy of the Hours. This does not mean that we need to offer a yearlong course in liturgical history and sacramental theology. Rather, liturgical education during the catechumenate should form the catechumen to see the liturgical-sacramental life as teaching men and women the art of self-giving love. Human beings are made for worship, and we are formed for this vocation through participation in the church's liturgies.

The remainder of this chapter will offer such a hypothesis, grounded in the *Catechism of the Catholic Church*. The goal is not just to repeat what the *Catechism* says about each sacrament. Instead, I hope to show a golden thread running through the sacramental system of Catholicism, one with pedagogical implications. In the sacramental liturgies of the church, all that is human is meant to become divine.

Why the Liturgy?

In the catechumenate, we'll need to answer this question: Why the liturgy? Such a question will inevitably surface, especially for Americans. My undergraduate students assume that what really matters is informality and sincerity in the act of worship. They have been catechized by American culture to presume that authentic prayer shouldn't be read from a book. It should be spontaneous, offered from the heart. They're partially right. It's good to be able to pray to God using our own speech. But liturgy isn't just about sincerity of heart. Liturgy *objectively* places us in relationship with the triune God so that we can *subjectively* respond. Liturgy is the concrete way that a human being comes to "participate" in the love of Christ. The fathers of the *Catechism* write, "It is this mystery of Christ that the Church proclaims and celebrates in her liturgy so that the faithful may live from it and bear witness to it in the world" (CCC 1068). Christian liturgy is not equivalent to prayer offered to God with other people. In this case, it would be possible for us to make up our own worship service or to belong to communities that celebrate the liturgy in a way that at least three or four of us like. The liturgy is instead the concrete, embodied, and complex series of signs whereby we learn to encounter Jesus Christ through the church.

During the RCIA, catechumens should thus learn to understand the liturgy as a concrete encounter with the mystery of God—Father, Son, and Holy Spirit. It's not an experience of abstract transcendence or a celebration of like-minded individuals who belong to the "club" of the church. Christian liturgy is participation in the life of God within the community of the church.

Participation in the life of God, of course, can sound rather abstract. What does that mean? Here, the *Catechism* offers a way to engage in such teaching: "In the liturgy of the Church, God the Father is blessed and adored as the source of all the blessings of creation and salvation with which he has blessed us in his Son, in order to give us the spirit of filial adoption" (CCC 1110). Liturgy necessitates a posture of blessing. And blessing requires us to see the world not as a space of accident or violence but as a space of gift.

Thus, liturgical formation commences with recognition of the gift that we have received in both creation and redemption. God loves us. God has poured out this love since the beginning of time. And we human beings have the capacity to offer a return gift of love to God.

Recognizing that the world is a gift, one given by God, is a hypothesis that we must offer to catechumens. Many of those who enter the catechumenate may not see the world as gift. They could be migrants who have suffered much in their journey to the United States; they could be children of sinful parents who abused them; they could be poor, hungry, and lonely. We can't just proclaim that the world is gift in a Pollyannaish manner, avoiding all reference to suffering. Instead, we must show them through the Scriptures, through our companionship, that God is love. We may even need to accompany the catechumen to recognize the presence of a God who has acted even in the midst of sorrow.

Learning gratitude is important. But in the church's liturgy we don't celebrate gratitude in general. In the liturgy, we celebrate a very specific story of salvation, fully revealed in the Son of the Father, Jesus Christ. This is not a story that remains locked in some distant past, "a long time ago." The *Catechism* clarifies:

> The Paschal mystery of Christ . . . cannot remain only in the past, because by his death he destroyed death, and all that Christ is—all that he did and suffered for all men—participates in the divine eternity, and so transcends all times while being made present in them all. The event of the Cross and Resurrection *abides* and draws everything toward life. (CCC 1085)

Jesus Christ is the Son of the Father, the Word who has become flesh. It is the Word made flesh who was born, suffered, died on the cross, and was raised from the dead. When Jesus ascended into heaven—his wounds transfigured through love—he never ceased being human. He remained the resurrected Word made flesh. *This* Jesus, this God who remains enfleshed in the Son, still acts in the church. The church's liturgy is not just a series of actions performed by the people, a priest, a cantor, a lector, or a communion minister. It is Christ, the glorified and risen Lord, acting among us through the people, priests, cantors, lectors, and communion ministers.

The presence of Christ in the liturgy is probably the best answer to "Why the liturgy?" When the church reads the Scriptures, when she encounters the sacrifice of Christ in the ministry of the priest, when she dwells with one another, she meets Jesus. And this Jesus is not just present in this church building. Through the liturgy, through lifting our voice in praise of the Father, we enter into the ceaseless liturgy that is celebrated in heaven.

This may be hard for many catechumens to believe. Perhaps, despite our best efforts, our liturgies are still bad! The singing could be off key. The priest and assembly who celebrate the liturgy could be less than holy. The lector could trip over the words of the Scriptures, and communion ministry might not be an occasion to offer Christ's Body and Blood to the People of God but a chance to prove one's importance among the assembly.

Thus, we must propose to the catechumen the following hypothesis: Christ is still present here! In the midst of a church embroiled in sexual abuse scandals, in a church where power sometimes defeats love, in a church where the mediocre is too often accepted, Jesus Christ becomes present. Love enters our lives. Thus, we go to Mass week-to-week not because we always like it. Instead, we go because there we dwell among the wounded, because we encounter our risen Savior there. We go with the hope that this church, no matter how wounded, might become the place where God will be all in all. Even if it's not perfect, God dwells among us.

How? Because, even in our weakness, God acts through the Holy Spirit. The *Catechism* states:

> The mission of the Holy Spirit in the liturgy of the church is to prepare the assembly to encounter Christ; to recall and manifest Christ to the faith of the assembly; to make the saving word of Christ present and active by his transforming power; and to make the gift of communion bear fruit in the Church. (CCC 1112)

In the liturgy, through the power of the Holy Spirit, we learn that not everything is about us. The formalized nature of the church's worship facilitates the work of the Holy Spirit. If every week we had to make up our own prayers, then we might come to the deadly conclusion that it was the sweetness of our poetic compositions that brought God down to us. Because *our* liturgy is beautiful, because *our* words are well chosen, because of *us*, God acts.

The grace of the Spirit, in every liturgy, is that God acts because God has promised to act. Not because we've deserved it or earned it. The Holy Spirit has been understood in the church as the love shared between the Father and the Son, and, in this sense, God's love comes no matter the worth of the recipient, because God is gift. No matter the awkwardness of the lector, God speaks in our midst through the breath of the Spirit. No matter how poor the pitch of the cantor, God speaks to us through hymns and canticles. No matter the holiness of a particular minister at the altar (and it's better to have a holy one), the Holy Spirit dwells among us transforming bread and wine into Christ's Body and Blood.

It is the "inspired" nature of liturgy that often has to be taught to catechumens. The Spirit doesn't always work with immediacy. We're not going to walk into Mass every week and say to ourselves, "There you are, Spirit." The working of the Holy Spirit in Mass is like the process of falling in love. At first, love might be immediate. We might experience instant and powerful affections when we're around our beloved, as we hold hands and enjoy passionate dates. But as time goes on, things change. Our love matures, and we learn to delight in spending time with our beloved in more mundane spaces. So too, we should prepare the catechumens that the work of the Spirit in the liturgy is often slow, more like spending time with one's beloved in a quiet living room rather than burning with passion on a dance floor.

The liturgy that has been passed on to us through the church is part of the work of the Holy Spirit. Through the hidden promptings of the Spirit, we have received the gift of the *ordo* of Mass, the eucharistic prayers, sacraments, chants, hymns, church buildings, and art. The liturgical life of the church comes to us as a gift, as capable of forming us over the course of our lifetime in the worshipful wisdom and divine blessing at the heart of Christian existence.

Why the Liturgical Year?

For many catechumens, the liturgical year is especially attractive. Human beings are grounded in time, aware that the change of seasons is linked closely to our contingency as persons. Advent gives way to Christmas, which becomes Ordinary Time, which becomes Lent, which leads to Easter, and on and on. Even children understand this, quickly learning as toddlers the names of the seasons.

The catechist should address the major seasons of the liturgical year as the catechumens encounter them. The liturgical year is best taught during the stage of the catechumenate by "practicing" the liturgical year in the context of the RCIA itself. Celebrations of the Word of God can introduce catechumens to the themes of each liturgical season while also giving them access to the chants, prayers, postures, and hymns that mark each season. In addition, the catechist should briefly describe the major solemnities and feasts of the church's year. Within the catechumenate, the sponsor should often share with the catechumen various ways of celebrating saint days not only in the church but also in the home.

Still, it's possible for catechumens to be confused about the nature of the liturgical year. The catechumen might believe that every time we celebrate Christmas or Easter, God is born and dies again. For such persons, the liturgical year becomes a "literal" reenactment of the life of Jesus Christ. The catechumen may also see the liturgical year as having a simple pedagogical function, teaching us about Jesus Christ. Both common fallacies are wrong. The liturgical year recalls and, through this recollection, invites us to participate in the mystery of Christ (CCC 1163).

Jesus Christ has acted in history as the Lord of heaven and earth. He will never be born again. He will never die again. But because Jesus Christ is the Word made flesh, because he is united closely to his Bride the church, Jesus Christ makes available the fruits of redemption for us here and now. The church has wisely parceled out various facets of Christ's life across the liturgical year. As human beings, we cannot contemplate all things at once. We need time as created and thus contingent beings. We become aware during each liturgical season how the Father, the Son, and the Holy Spirit have acted in history. And we are slowly formed to see how God will act, in a similar way, among us today.

The liturgical year is key to grasping the sacramental system of the church. God has acted in the past, acts now in the present, and will act in the future. The liturgical year and the sacraments are not "magical" rites or "ancient" myths of an ever-returning God. Rather, the liturgical year and the sacraments are the privileged ways that God pilgrims with his church through history.

It's important to meet these potential confusions of the catechumens head on. When we do, we give to the catechumens a valuable instrument for the spiritual life. They will come to see how their relationship with Christ is lived out through the cycle of time, how the Father patiently forms us to adore Jesus Christ through the Spirit year-by-year. Sponsors and catechists alike should share how their own relationship with Jesus has been deepened through celebrating the liturgical year.

Why the Liturgy of the Hours?

In this book, I will more formally treat the Liturgy of the Hours in the context of the period of mystagogy. Still, early in the catechumenate, we should tell catechumens about the Liturgy of the Hours, perhaps giving them a copy of *Shorter Christian Prayer*. After all, repetition is the mother of learning. The Liturgy of the Hours, especially for more mature catechumens, can be an occasion to encounter the mystery of Christ throughout the course of the day. The *Catechism* states:

> The mystery of Christ, his Incarnation and Passover, which we celebrate in the Eucharist especially at the Sunday assembly, permeates and transfigures the time of each day, through the celebration of the Liturgy of the Hours, "the divine office." This celebration, faithful to the apostolic exhortations to "pray constantly," is "so devised that the whole course of the day and night is made holy by the praise of God." (CCC 1174)

The liturgical year shows us how the seasons of the year may be transfigured in Christ. But in the Liturgy of the Hours, we come to encounter Jesus Christ as permeating every dimension of time. Christ comes to us in the middle of night, as we rise to praise the creator of light and dark alike. Christ comes to us in the morning, as we praise God for the rising of the Son. Christ comes to us as the sun sets, as we consecrate once more our whole day to God.

Catechumens will discover the power of the Liturgy of the Hours most easily in our common prayer with one another. And commitment to this liturgy will be essential to conducting a serious, committed approach to mystagogy.

Why the Sacraments?

As a Catholic who grew up in the American South, I was often met with somewhat suspicious questions from my Protestant classmates about Catholicism. One of the most prominent involved the sacraments: why did Catholics put so much emphasis on the grace made available in the sacraments? Doesn't God give grace outside of the church's prayer?

The answer is yes. The church's sacramental system is not the exclusive way that God works in the lives of men and women. Catechists need to be careful to ground any conversation about the sacraments during the catechumenate in a proper understanding of grace. As the *Catechism* defines it, "Grace is *favor, the free and undeserved help* that God gives us to respond to his call to become children of God, adoptive sons, partakers of divine nature and of eternal life" (CCC 1996). The church understands different types of grace, such as sanctifying grace, which is received in baptism. Sanctifying (also called deifying or habitual) is that grace that allows us to enter into relationship with God, bestowing on us a new identity as sons and daughters of the Father. This is the grace that forever changes our identity—for this reason, a Catholic can never be "unbaptized." But the church also speaks about actual grace, particular moments of divine intervention in the life of an individual that is part of the pilgrimage toward holiness.

The sacraments have an important role to play in enabling us to participate fully in the life of God, living out the fruits of this sanctifying grace. The sacraments are not magic, saving men and women even if they don't want to be saved. You can't kill puppies, go to the sacrament of penance, and then kill puppies again. Getting the sacraments right requires attention to a clear definition that cuts across each of the sacraments:

> The sacraments are efficacious signs of grace, instituted by Christ and entrusted to the Church, by which divine life is dispensed

to us. The visible rites by which the sacraments are celebrated signify and make present the graces proper to each sacrament. They bear fruit in those who receive them with the required dispositions. (CCC 1131)

The sacraments are "efficacious signs." This phrase presumes that the sacraments "communicate" something to the human person about God, while also working to bring the human being into a deeper relationship with God. The sacraments are signs that involve materiality. They consist of words and matter. But as signs, they don't just refer to themselves. Water is not just water. Oil is not just oil. They point to something else. And because they point to something else, they are efficacious. They bring about grace.

What do they point to? The *Catechism* states, "The mysteries of Christ's life are the foundations of what he would henceforth dispense in the sacraments, through the ministers of the Church, for 'what was visible in the Savior has passed over into his mysteries'" (CCC 1115). Everything that Jesus Christ did on earth was salvific. He healed the sick. His preaching, the power of his speech, announced the Good News that love alone is credible. He fed his disciples, at the Last Supper, with his Body and Blood. And now through the sacraments of the church, Jesus is active again here and now. When the church baptizes or confirms, it is not the minister alone who acts. It is Christ.

The church does not claim this to control Jesus, as if to say, "We have Christ, and you don't!" Rather, the church has this power only because of who she is, the Mystical Body of Christ. Christ acts in the church through the sacraments because Jesus is always and everywhere closely wedded to the church. Over time, the church gradually recognized that there were seven of these sacraments instituted by Christ. The church can make decisions about the rites of these sacraments because, through her, Christ acts.

The important point to underline with the sacraments is the presence of Christ made available through efficacious signs. Matter matters. As human beings, we are not simply intellectual creatures. We don't experience salvation as a moment of mental insight—"I am saved!" Instead, as embodied creatures, we are both material and spiritual. It's not enough for me to think about love toward my spouse. Sometimes, I need to bring home roses, which become a tangible sign of my love. The roses are efficacious signs, bringing about a deeper union between the two of us. Our love has a concrete sign to ground itself in.

Thus, it's not that the sacraments are the way that the church controls grace. Rather, the sacraments are like divine roses given to human beings. God doesn't just say, "I love you, once upon a time . . . " God's love is efficacious here and now. Each of the sacraments, as we'll see, shows a particular facet of God's love for us, while also allowing us to participate in God's very life. That's what the church means by saying that the sacraments "make present the graces proper to each sacrament." Each sacrament is God acting among us in a particular way.

For this reason, sacramental grace is best understood not as a "quantity" of divine love given to us but as a rite that facilitates a relationship between God and the church, including each member of Christ's Body. The *Catechism* states:

> "Sacramental grace" is the grace of the Holy Spirit, given by Christ and proper to each sacrament. The Spirit heals and transforms those who receive him by conforming them to the Son of God. The fruit of the sacramental life is that the Spirit of adoption makes the faithful partakers in the divine nature by uniting them in a living union with the only Son, the Savior. (CCC 1129)

The sacraments accompany the church and each person throughout history. When the church celebrates the sacrament of the Eucharist, for example, the Spirit is given to the whole church, forming the church in eucharistic love. At the same time, as we eat and drink Christ's Body and Blood, our very bodies participate in divine life. We grow closer to Jesus, becoming ever more divine.

When teaching this to the catechumens, we should think about sacramental grace as the way that God accompanies each of us throughout our lives. The triune God has not left us orphans in the world. But over the course of our lifetimes, God enables us to enter more deeply into relationship with the Lord of life. An important passage to highlight in the *Catechism* is the correspondence between the natural and supernatural life in the sacraments: "The seven sacraments touch all the stages and all the important moments of Christian life: they give birth and increase, healing and mission to the Christian's life of faith. There is thus a certain resemblance between the stages of natural life and the stages of the spiritual life" (CCC 1210). From birth to death, God is here with us. And God greets us in a way appropriate to each stage of our life.

Still, to receive the fruits of the sacraments requires attuning ourselves to the proper dispositions. Forming catechumens in these sacramental dispositions is an important task of the catechumenate. A danger of the sacramental system in the church is that we emphasize the "efficaciousness" of the sacrament without due attention to a sacrament's "fruitfulness." When the church baptizes someone in the name of the Father, the Son, and the Holy Spirit, it works. But for one to receive the fruits of the sacraments, one must be disposed to do so. The entire RCIA depends on this assumption—we must be disposed or attuned to participate fully in the sacramental life.

Thus, it's not enough to just teach the definition of each sacrament. During the catechumenate, we need to attune the catechumen to each of the dispositions or capacities necessary for receiving the sacrament. Going to penance requires a disposition of conversion, of constantly seeking God's mercy. Participation in the Eucharist requires a disposition of desire, longing to feast at the banquet of the living God. The overarching goal of formation into the church's teaching around the sacraments should be to "show" how the sacraments enable the human being to become a worshipful offering to God throughout our lives.

Why the Sacraments of Initiation?

Within the catechumenate, it is most essential to spend significant time on the sacraments of initiation. For one, the catechumen is preparing to receive these sacraments during the Easter Vigil.

But even more important, "The sacraments of Christian initiation—Baptism, Confirmation, and the Eucharist—lay the *foundation* of every Christian life" (CCC 1212). One can think about these sacraments as teaching nearly everything that a catechumen needs to know about the Christian life in order to adore the living God.

The sacrament of baptism consists of a series of signs including water, sacred chrism, invocation of the Trinity, a white garment, and a candle. Familiarity with these signs may be facilitated easily through attending an infant baptism at a parish. The catechumens should encounter the "stuff" of baptism, seeing the rite unfold before their eyes.

Encountering the signs of baptism may be enough during the stage of the catechumenate. But, it may be worthwhile to think more deeply about what each of the signs provokes. For human beings, water is a source of both life and death. Through water, we are cleansed. Yet, through water, entire cities can be destroyed. Anyone who has thought for a moment that they were drowning knows that water refreshes and kills. In addition, a light shining out in the darkness is not only comforting. It can save. Some years ago, my spouse and I had the experience of driving in pitch darkness on a snowy, mountainous road, afraid that if we skidded off, we'd tumble to our death. We felt rescued, liberated from death, when we encountered a streetlight that showed us that there was no cliff—just a small ditch.

But our reflection on the signs cannot remain at the level of the material. Christian liturgy takes up the natural dimension of human religiosity, transforming it through an encounter with Jesus Christ. So we have to show how our celebration of baptism is linked to the history of salvation. For each of the sacraments, there is a "kerygma" or proclamation of salvation that can be told. The blessing prayer for the Easter Vigil is especially important in discovering the baptismal kerygma: God quells the chaos of water at creation, God leads Noah safely across the waters of the flood, God parts the Red Sea, God shepherds Israel through the Jordan River, Jesus is baptized, and water flows from the side of Christ at his death. Baptism allows us to participate in this history of salvation.

What, though, does baptism do? Answering this question from the example of infant baptism is important for the catechumen. For baptism is not earned but comes as a freely given grace, entering the child from the first moment of its breath into the love of the Father, the Son, and the Holy Spirit. The grace of baptism is the conferral of a new identity on the recently baptized Christian. The one being baptized does not need to have a perfect faith, totally convicted by Jesus Christ. Instead, it is important to emphasize that "it is only within the faith of the Church that each of the faithful can believe. The faith required for Baptism is not a perfect and mature faith, but a beginning that is called to develop" (CCC 1253). The entire communion of saints provides what each newly baptized Christian lacks relative to faith. Baptism saves by entering one into the life of the church.

Many catechumens will find this teaching difficult. In modernity, we have been taught that we are isolated individuals, monads who can depend entirely on ourselves. The church has a different understanding of the human person that is proposed in the sacrament of baptism. From the beginning, we are made for relationship. My faith exists only in relationship to the church's faith. When I can't pray, when I can't believe, that doesn't mean my faith has disappeared. It means that I need to rely even more on the whole church, the whole communion of saints. Sponsors and catechists should speak about experiences when they have struggled with Christian faith, relying not on their own power but on the faith of the entire church.

Teaching the sacrament of baptism, during the catechumenate, should especially highlight the fruits of the sacraments. During RCIA, there is a danger that the catechumen will understand his or her baptism as a "graduation" from the RCIA "program." That's not what happens. The *Catechism* mentions the following fruits for baptism: sins are forgiven, one becomes a new creature in Christ, one enters into Christ's Body—incorporated into the unity of all Christians, and one receives a sacramental mark that forever marks one as a Christian (what the church calls a character).

I would recommend that we first introduce catechumens to the last fruit, the indelible mark. Baptism is a total change of identity, a transformation of who we are. We no longer exist for ourselves, but when the priest plunges us into the water of salvation, baptizing us in the name of the Father, the Son, and the Holy Spirit, something has changed. I am not "Tim" or "Mary" alone. Rather, I am forever united to Christ and thus to the church. My sins are forgiven because to be so close to Jesus, to have him become part of my very identity, means encountering the healing mercy of God. I enter into the church, sharing my new identity not just with God but also with all those who have become my brothers and sisters in Christ. As a member of this Body of Christ, I have a new responsibility to make the invisible spiritual mark of baptism evident in the world:

> Incorporated into the Church by Baptism, the faithful have received the sacramental character that consecrates them for Christian religious worship. The baptismal seal enables and commits Christians to serve God by a vital participation in the holy liturgy of the Church and to exercise their baptismal priesthood by the witness of holy lives and practical charity. (CCC 1273)

The proper disposition required for fruitful reception of baptism is awareness of the remarkable transformation possible in Christ. We must cultivate a desire within the catechumen to become a temple of the living God, the embodiment of divine love in the world. Participating in the fruits of baptism begins from a desire for a new identity in Christ, one that has global consequences for how we live. For this reason, learning to dwell in the community of the church, to share our lives with one another is not optional. Yes, we must become sons and daughters of the Father through sharing in Christ's life. But, that means that we become brothers and sisters with one another.

Baptism, thus, offers us a hypothesis. We are not made to be self-made individuals. That's the root of sin. Instead, we are made for communion, for relationship with Jesus Christ and his church.

Confirmation is the second sacrament of initiation. As many catechists know, it is an especially hard sacrament to teach. The sacrament of confirmation was originally celebrated immediately following baptism, closely linked to the anointing with chrism and the hand-laying of the bishop. But through a series of historical accidents, it was separated from baptism, celebrated when the bishop was able to visit a parish. In the twentieth century, the sacrament of confirmation began to be celebrated in mid-adolescence, after the reception of the Eucharist. Because of this, for many in the church, the sacrament of confirmation is when individual Christians make baptismal faith their own.

This understanding of confirmation as a time to "prove one's faith" is not sufficient. As the *Catechism* clarifies, "by the sacrament of Confirmation, [the baptized] are more perfectly bound to the Church and are enriched with a special strength of the Holy Spirit. Hence they are, as true witnesses of Christ, more strictly obliged to spread and defend the faith by word and deed" (CCC 1285). Confirmation is a sacrament of maturation. But the mature disciple is not one who has examined every dimension of the Creed, proved understanding of it, and then graduated. Rather, confirmation is the perfection of baptism, a fresh outpouring of grace that is ordered toward the completion of baptism.

Because of the link between baptism and confirmation, it is probably wise to teach the two sacraments during the RCIA at the same time, while recognizing that in a particular diocese the confirmation of already-baptized children may take place anywhere between the ages of seven and sixteen. Some dioceses have a "restored order," celebrating confirmation before the reception of the Eucharist around seven or eight years old. Theologians and pastoral leaders need to figure out whether this strange diversity of ages makes sense and whether the restored order is more prudent as a strategy for evangelization. But the catechumenate should not be introduced into this debate. It's enough to focus on how the catechumen will experience confirmation, as closely linked to baptism, as an outpouring of the Holy Spirit.

The signs of confirmation include the sacred chrism, the profession of faith, the extending of hands over the catechumens, and the sign of peace. Emphasis during the catechumenate should focus on the sacred chrism and the extension of hands, which are both linked closely to the baptismal nature of the sacrament. In receiving the sacred chrism, as well as through the extension of hands, the confirmand is invited to share completely in the priesthood of Jesus Christ. Christ, after all, isn't Jesus's family name. Instead, Jesus is the anointed one, the one who has received a full outpouring of the Holy Spirit. In confirmation, the confirmand receives an outpouring of the Spirit, becoming an *alter Christus* or another Christ.

The emphasis of the sacrament of confirmation is on the vocation of the Christian to witness to the reality of divine love in the world (CCC 1309). Confirmation is an apostolic sacrament, sending one forth to witness to God's love in the world. That's why the ordinary minister of the sacrament is the bishop, who is the living manifestation of the apostles in the church. Speaking about vocation or God's call is pivotal to preparation for the sacrament of confirmation. Baptism does not simply conform one to Christ, saving the individual. Instead, the person who has met Jesus Christ through the Spirit is called to share this love with the world. The kerygma of confirmation should be oriented toward the apostolic nature of confirmation. Notice in the gospels that Jesus comes to announce the Good News that the kingdom of God is at hand. In Jesus Christ, the powers of the world have met their match. And thus, the Christian is to go forth to every corner and crevice of creation, making this fact known through word and deed. The destiny of the Christian is mission.

Chrism is an appropriate sign for this permanent, total transformation of the person. When my son was baptized, he received a postbaptismal anointing of sacred chrism (not the sacrament of confirmation!). For days after, he smelled like this chrism. That's what confirmation should do for the Christian. We are to become God's smelly ones (smelling good, of course). Each person who encounters us should recognize immediately that there is something different about us. That's our vocation. Confirmation seals this vocation.

The food that sustains us in this vocation is the Eucharist. The temptation during catechesis is to focus immediately on the "how" of the Eucharist. We want to answer the question related to the transformation of bread and wine into Christ's Body and Blood. For a mature believer, this can be a salutary exercise. But such a question does not get to the heart of the Eucharist—why does this sacrament matter so much? Why is it the source and summit of Christian life?

The *Catechism* answers this foundational question:

> The Eucharist is the heart and the summit of the Church's life, for in it Christ associates his Church and all her members with his sacrifice of praise and thanksgiving offered once for all on the cross to his Father; by this sacrifice he pours out the graces of salvation on his Body which is the Church. (CCC 1407)

The Eucharist is about Christ's sacrifice, love unto the end, now celebrated from the heart of the church.

Each of us longs for a total and absolute love. As young children, we wish that our parents could provide this love. But as children, we quickly learn that they cannot. The rest of our lives is often taken up with searching for this love through friends, co-workers, and romantic interests. No relationship can complete us. There is something more we hope for.

As creatures, we have been made for a total love. And God is the source of this sacrificial love. In creation, God loved us by forming us in his image and likeness. God loved Israel, rescuing them from slavery, freeing them by means of the first Passover meal and the parting of the Red Sea. God fed Israel in the desert, communed with Israel in the temple sacrifice. God was patient with Israel, promising that there would be a new covenant sealed with a great feast in which all nations would be invited. And in the fullness of time, the Word became flesh and loved us, flesh-to-flesh. Jesus ate with sinners and saints. He transformed water into wine, giving us a foretaste of the great feast promised by the prophets. On the night before he was betrayed, he loved us unto the end by offering a new covenant. In this new covenant, sealed on the cross, the human body becomes the site of total and absolute love. And this love unto the end conquered the loneliness at the heart of the human condition. It conquered sin and death, for on the third day, God raised Jesus from the dead. The disciples on the road to Emmaus encountered the presence of our living God, recognizing him in the breaking of the bread. Their hearts were healed through encountering Jesus in the Eucharist. And in every parish throughout the world, we too are given this total love, the flesh and blood of our Lord. We eat total love so that we might become this love for the world.

This is the ultimate hypothesis offered by the Eucharist. God loved us unto the end. God makes this love available to us here and now, so that we can become this love for the life of the world. A catechumen who has learned the grammar of the church's liturgical prayer should not be surprised how the Eucharist works. When we celebrate the memorial of Christ's sacrifice, the fruits of this sacrifice become available to us because God has pitched his tent among us. When we teach the doctrine of transubstantiation, we must teach it within the context of this narrative. Bread and wine are transformed into Christ's Body and Blood. God gives everything, not holding anything back. But in order to feed us, God gives himself in a way that we human beings can eat and drink—through the signs of bread and wine.

The fruits of the Eucharist pertain to participation in Christ's sacrifice. Eating Christ's Body and Blood, we receive nourishment from Christ himself. It is fitting that God has chosen to feed us. The signs of bread and wine are important to the sacrament. The Eucharist is the great banquet of love, nourishing us over the course of our lifetime. The more that catechists and sponsors can share with catechumens how the Eucharist has sustained them, the more open the catechumen will be to the fruit of eucharistic communion.

Because the Eucharist nourishes us with Christ's love, it also heals us of sin (CCC 1394). We must form catechumens to long for the Eucharist, to long for love itself. The Eucharist does not erase sin magically but instead restores us to a deeper longing to dwell in the presence of God. It's like a couple having a date night. Having a date doesn't erase the effects of any arguments that the couple has had over the course of the week. But by spending time with one another, the couple learns to desire their friendship anew. So too in the Eucharist—we learn to once again desire total union with Christ.

The Eucharist also fruitfully produces a union among members of Christ's Body, the church (CCC 1396). The sacrifice of praise offered by the church restores the communion of men and women in Christ. The ironic part of the Eucharist is that as we participate in the sacrifice of the Mass, our deepest longing for love is restored to us. We want total love with our parents, with our friends, and with our spouse. Such love is not possible unless it begins through the total and absolute love of Christ. We receive infinite love so that we might become this love, so that we might experience this love in every dimension of our lives.

During the catechumenate, much of what we say about the Eucharist must be related to desire. The catechumens cannot yet savor the sweetness of our eucharistic Lord. Thus, in teaching the Eucharist, it is good to underline once more why they are dismissed before the Liturgy of the Eucharist. When they are able to receive Holy Communion, to savor the fullness of love, they will be entirely united not just to God but also to all of us. It's okay to long for this.

Sharing the essential biblical themes of the Eucharist is important. Teaching them how to pray the Mass is key. But our sacramental catechesis around the Eucharist must have as its end the proposal of the only hypothesis that can answer the desire at the heart of being human—love unto the end. The Eucharist is that divine presence that sustains us while also bestowing on the church an icon of who she is to become. We don't always live up to our eucharistic identity. The catechist has to recognize this lest our discussion of the Eucharist seems Pollyannaish. There are hypocrites, sinners, and liars among us. But because of the love of Christ, because of the power of the Spirit, because of the presence of Christ available in the Eucharist, there is hope. Love will win. The Eucharist is the pledge of eternal life, that which gives us hope in this age.

The sacraments of initiation thus reveal the entirety of the Christian life. We are made for total union with Christ, to become sons and daughters of the Father. In our new identity as priests, prophets, and royal figures, we are called by the Spirit to share the Good News throughout the world that love has won. And on our journey, we are nourished by receiving this love through savoring Christ's Body and Blood each Sunday not as individuals but as the whole church, called to become a city of loving praise. Because of the comprehensive nature of the sacraments of initiation, they could serve as the very basis of a curriculum for the entire catechumenate.

Why the Sacraments of Healing?

The sacraments of initiation bring us toward maturation, as we move from those reborn in the waters of baptism to the mature who are fed with Christ's Body and Blood. But both the natural and Christian lives do not consist of exclusive growth. In every life, there is diminishment. As we grow older, we discover that we are not ready for the fullness of wisdom, suffering from a foolishness that keeps us from living well. We learn our limitations—such as when I learned in eighth grade that, with a height of five foot nothing, I was not destined to play for the Boston Celtics. We also get sick, evidence that we human beings are not creatures that exist in some eternal realm. We are contingent. And eventually, we will contract that illness that brings us to death's door.

Because of the contingent nature of human life, there are also sacraments of healing (CCC 1420). Through baptism, confirmation, and the Eucharist, we experience union with the living God. But just because we have "experienced" this union, this gift of love, doesn't mean that we'll always love perfectly in return. And the communion that we experience in the church is deeply challenged by the presence of sickness and death, when it may seem to us like we're cut off from communion all together.

Just as Jesus comes to us in the sacrament of baptism, confirmation, and the Eucharist, our Lord is also present to us in the sacrament of penance and reconciliation. Likely, the catechumens will have some vision of this sacrament, which may make understanding of the gift of the sacrament difficult. Having watched movies that reference the Catholic Church, they have surely seen penitents pour out their worst sins anonymously in a dark box in a church. They might be scared of the sacrament.

The *Catechism* attempts to correct this misunderstanding by recognizing the variety of names given to the sacrament. It is called the sacrament of conversion, penance, confession, forgiveness, and reconciliation. The list of names in the *Catechism* demonstrates the order of importance.

The sacrament of penance is first and foremost an occasion for conversion. Conversion is at the heart of the Gospel. For those of us initiated into Jesus Christ, we recognize the depths of love to which we are called. And, for this reason, we are equally cognizant of where we have missed the mark.

I often think about this relative to my career as a professor. Having studied theology for fifteen years, having learned to develop lengthy arguments over the course of papers, having taught in the classroom for eight years, I'm super-aware of how I can be intellectually lazy, can be too quick to attend to complex arguments, and can forget how much work teaching can be. I know when I've missed the mark to my calling as a professor.

The sacrament of penance is thus a requirement for any Christian who understands the meaning of baptism. But, unlike my life as a professor, penance is not just the result of our human recognition. The Spirit is involved in the act of conversion (CCC 1428). Encountering Christ the healer, the one who calls us to enter fully into the kingdom of God, we are also "shaken by the horror and weight of sin and begin . . . to fear offending God by sin and being separated from him. The human heart is converted by looking upon him whom our sins have pierced" (CCC 1432).

The essence of the sacrament of penance and reconciliation is a desire for conversion. This disposition toward conversion is not expressed through unspoken or unshared regret. When my son is really sorry, when he recognizes that he has not loved well, he'll often come up to me and give me a hug. In the church, our bodies are involved in conversion. We fast, pray, and give alms. We admit our faults to our husband or wife, our brother and sister, and our coworker. We abstain from meat on Fridays during Lent. We give up technology so that we can focus on our relationship with God. These bodily practices orient us toward a life of conversion, one whereby we desire God through the exercise of our bodies. During the catechumenate, even before we teach the sacrament of penance and reconciliation, we should give the catechumens access to practices of penance.

The sacrament of penance and reconciliation takes this disposition of conversion and places it within the context of a liturgical rite. The rite involves four parts: contrition, confession, an act of penance, and absolution. During the RCIA, it is most important to deal with these four parts of the sacrament, teaching the catechumen to participate fully, consciously, and actively in this rite. A priest, deacon, catechist, or sponsor should go over the various parts of this rite. In addition, the catechumen should attend a parish penance service during Advent or Lent, to see how this rite is not reducible to the private conversation in the box with a priest. The logic of the rite of penance and reconciliation is a movement from hearing the call to conversion in the Scriptures to our confession of sins to penance and then to absolution.

Much has already been said about contrition. During the catechumenate, it will be important to form catechumens to see contrition not as an occasion for excessive shame but as a response to love. Catechumens, as they enter into Christian life, will most likely recognize the gap between the divine love they are experiencing in the church and their former ways of life. They'll become aware of the ways that they, for example, caused their marriage to end. They may recognize their own reliance on consumer goods for human happiness. They'll see the weakness of their own wills, perhaps failing to pray or long for God like they want to. Catechists and sponsors should not dismiss this "guilt." But they should direct it toward a response of radical love. Early on in the catechumenate, a good catechist will introduce catechumens to the parable of the Prodigal Son. The abuse of freedom on the parts of the younger and older sons is important. But it's also pivotal to note the festive reception of the younger son on the part of so merciful a Father: "The beautiful robe, the ring, and the festive banquet are symbols of that new life—pure, worthy, and joyful—of anyone who returns to God and to the bosom of his family, which is the Church" (CCC 1439). The rite of penance and reconciliation is not about shame. It's about offering the return gift of love of a wounded heart to the living God.

That's why, during the catechumenate, we should be careful in drawing too clear a distinction between venial and mortal sins. Venial sins, we know, are things like being angry with the driver in the parking lot. Mortal sins include adultery and murder. The latter cut us off from communion with God and the church, while the former are those daily transgressions that are healed through weekly attendance at Mass, daily prayer, and care for the poor. We don't want the catechumen to focus too intensely on assessing the venial or mortal nature of his or her sins. Instead, we want them to see that because God is love, because this love has been poured out in the human family, we are made for something more than sin. It is an act of worship to celebrate the rite of penance and reconciliation—one that heals us of all sin. The sacramental life necessitates that we approach the Eucharist, communion with the living God, ready to receive this total love. That's why, after baptism, we should frequent the sacrament of penance and reconciliation.

The rite of penance and reconciliation also includes the confession of sins. It's hard for us to name to anyone—a priest, a neighbor, even our spouse—where we've missed the mark. But the act of confessing our sins is an occasion of worship, of admitting to God that we are not the Creator but a creature in need of grace. The sacrament of penance and reconciliation thus requires self-knowledge. We have to know where we have missed the mark, what precisely is the sin that we have done. Introducing catechumens to a process of examining their consciences will be key to forming them to make a good confession. If we spend time each day contemplating where we have failed to love God and neighbor, the act of confessing our sins to a priest will become easier for us to do.

The confession of sins, in particular, will generate resistance among many catechumens. They may say something like, "Why can't I confess my sins directly to God rather than to a priest?" Of course, one can and will confess one's sins to God. But in confessing our sins to a priest, we're recognizing that sin is never a private affair. Baptized into Christ, we belong to the communion of the church. Our sins hurt the entire body of believers too. Examples will help in this regard. When I lie to my neighbor, I'm not just harming my neighbor. I'm introducing violence into the world, a sense of distrust that ruptures the communion that is the destiny of men and women in Christ. By confessing my sins to a priest, who is acting as a representative of Christ, I'm acknowledging that my faults have global effects.

That's why penance is part of the sacrament of confession. In sin, the order of divine love is disrupted. And something has to be done to make this up. Ideally, the penance should also be healing for the penitent. The penance isn't really a punishment as much as an occasion to involve our entire bodies in the act of returning to God. The *Catechism* notes:

> The penance the confessor imposes must take into account the penitent's personal situation and must seek his spiritual good. It must correspond as far as possible with the gravity and nature of the sins committed. It can consist of prayer, an offering, works of mercy, service of neighbor, voluntary self-denial, sacrifices, and above all the patient acceptance of the cross we must bear. Such penances help configure us to Christ, who alone expiated our sins once for all. They allow us to become co-heirs with the risen Christ. (CCC 1460)

Take someone who easily becomes angry with others. An appropriate penance would be for the person to pray an Our Father or Hail Mary every time he or she is tempted to react with anger within the next week.

Now, most of us cannot control the penances that are given in the confessional. But we should emphasize in teaching penance that giving our will over to a penance, even a minimal one, is itself salutary and that the act of penance, of practicing self-discipline or self-denial, can certainly go beyond what the priest suggests. There is nothing wrong with saying more than three Hail Marys and three Our Fathers. Remember, the sacrament of penance and reconciliation is always a return gift of love.

The sacrament also involves a moment of absolution. Sin has not just offended God but cut us off from communion with the church. Absolution restores this communion, bringing us back into relationship with Christ and the church. The absolution given by the priest, of course, is not his own. He's not saying, "I forgive you." But through the sacrament of penance and reconciliation, the priest becomes a sign of God's love for the sinner.

Teaching the sacrament of penance, as one can see, is thus not just a matter of telling catechumens about the sacrament. Rather, there needs to be a real spiritual formation, leading the catechumens to desire conversion, to see the confession of sins as worship, to practice penance, and to recognize that sin cuts us off from communion with the whole church.

The Christian needs healing not only from particular sins but from the effect of sin on the human person, evident in illness. Illness is often an occasion of loneliness, something that cuts us off from communion with the entire human family. In the last days of my grandmother's life, she was radically alone even when she was in the presence of other people. Suffering the ravages of Alzheimer's, she could no longer speak except in half-formed syllables. She was constantly afraid that someone had come to do her harm. This woman, once so strong, vivacious, and talkative, became an infant in the body of an eighty-year-old woman.

Illness also brings us into a crisis relative to our relationship with God. How many of those suffering from cancer have cried out to God, "Why me?" How many who have endured the horrors of mental illness or nerve disease have wondered to themselves, "How long, O Lord?" Because our God has entered radically into the human condition, even in such loneliness as experienced on the cross, Jesus Christ is there to encounter us.

Jesus Christ comes to heal us in our suffering. The sacrament of the anointing of the sick is important to this healing. This sacrament is not a "guaranteed" healing from the physical effects of the illness. Many of those who have received this anointing, including my grandmother, still died from their disease. But this sacrament gives to the ill person the strength to consecrate their illness, to allow it to be offered to God as a sacrifice of love. As the *Catechism* notes:

> By the grace of this sacrament the sick person receives the strength and gift of uniting himself more closely to Christ's Passion: in a certain way he is *consecrated* to bear fruit by configuration to the Savior's redemptive Passion. Suffering, a consequence of original sin, acquires a new meaning; it becomes a participation in the saving work of Jesus. (CCC 1521)

Through the anointing, the suffering of the person with illness becomes a liturgical offering. This illness, this suffering, manifests to the world that divine love and blessing are found even in the midst of suffering. The ill person performs a ministry for the entire People of God. Everything, including our illness, our frailty, can be offered in love to the triune God.

Catechumens should become familiar with the signs of this sacrament, including the Word of God, the laying on of hands, and the anointing with oil. Emphasis should be placed on the communion, the touching of flesh to flesh in the sacrament. Illness cuts us off from communion with God and one another. And through the ministry of the church, communion is restored.

In this sacrament, one can see the dignity of the human person. We want to hide the sick and elderly, to put them in nursing communities apart from the rest of society. But the church refuses to reduce the sick and elderly to their age or illness. That's why the anointing of the sick should be celebrated in public—whether in a hospital surrounded by family or in the context of a eucharistic liturgy in a parish. It's only natural in preparing catechumens to understand this sacrament that we invite them to spend time with the sick in our parish.

We should emphasize to catechumens that the anointing of the sick is not reserved to those who are dying. It should be given to all those who are suffering from serious illness. This sacrament may be given many times over the course of the illness. Nonetheless, there is an anointing that is proper to the end of our life, what the church calls *viaticum*. Here, the sick receives an anointing and participates in the Eucharist. As the *Catechism* notes, "The sacrament of Christ once dead and now risen, the Eucharist is here the sacrament of passing over from death to life, from this world to the Father" (CCC 1524). Especially at the moment of death, the occasion in which we pass beyond the vale of this world to life with the Father, Christ is there.

It is appropriate to introduce catechumens to funerals in the context of discussing the anointing of the sick and viaticum. A funeral is not a sacrament, which does not mean it's insignificant. The church defines a funeral as a sacramental, "instituted for the sanctification of certain ministries of the Church, certain states of life, a great variety of circumstances in Christian life, and the use of many things helpful to man" (CCC 1668). As a sacramental, it does not effect grace but instead consecrates even the act of dying to God.

Part of the formation of the catechumen should include attendance at a funeral within the parish. Here, the catechumen will discover the whole meaning of the sacramental life of the church. The *Catechism* states:

> The Church who, as Mother, has borne the Christian sacramentally in her womb during his earthly pilgrimage, accompanies him at his journey's end, in order to surrender him "into the Father's hands." She offers to the Father, in Christ, the child of his grace, and she commits to the earth, in hope, the seed of the body that will rise in glory. This offering is fully celebrated in the Eucharistic sacrifice; the blessings before and after Mass are sacramentals. (CCC 1683)

The one who has died in Christ has not suffered a defeat. He or she has not been cut off from communion. For us Christians, death is not the end. Each time we celebrate the eucharistic sacrifice in the church, we're not the only ones there. The entire communion of saints is present, including our beloved dead, adoring the living God.

The sacraments of healing thus show us how even our diminishments, how sin and illness, can become occasions to worship the living God. By confessing our sins, undertaking penance, we are restored to communion with Christ and the church. And by receiving the oil of salvation in the sacrament of the sick, we consecrate our serious illness to God. Christ nourishes us even in our diminishment, allowing growth to occur in the most unexpected of places.

Why the Sacraments at the Service of Communion?

In addition to the sacraments of initiation and healing, there are two sacraments oriented toward a sanctifying grace given for the salvation of the human family: matrimony and holy orders. These sacraments are at the service of communion. Both involve a moment of consecration.

In the context of the catechumenate, more time should probably be spent on the sacrament of matrimony since most catechumens will have greater familiarity and personal experience with this state of life. Human beings know the thrill of falling in love. We also know what it is like to belong to the institution of a family, sharing a life in common with other men and women.

The sacrament of matrimony consecrates the mundaneness of human love and family life, something so radically human, to God. This consecration begins in the Scriptures. In the beginning, man and woman were created by God for love. When Genesis describes Adam and Eve as created in the image and likeness of God, it is proclaiming that men and women are made for communion. Marriage and procreation were part of the way that men and women would sanctify the created order, expressing their relationship with God. The tragedy of the garden is that the communion of Adam and Eve was broken through sin. Blame, anger, and divorce enter into the story. Jesus Christ, in his teaching on adultery and divorce, comes to restore this communion between man and woman. In the kingdom of God, man and woman will remain faithful to each other unto the end, once again manifesting to the world what it means to have been created in the image and likeness of God.

This thread of fidelity between man and woman is not the only aspect of the nuptial or marriage kerygma. In the Prophets, we hear about the covenant of love between God and Israel. This covenant is understood as a marriage—one that Israel has not always been faithful to. God promises throughout the Old Testament to offer a new covenant to Israel. Israel will become the bride who gives everything to God, who is faithful because she loves God unto the end. This new covenant is evident in the New Testament. Jesus's transformation of water into wine at the wedding of Cana inaugurates this new wedding feast. Traditionally, the bridegroom would supply the wine, and now Jesus proclaims in this sign, "I am the Bridegroom." From the side of Christ on the cross, blood and water flow forth. Just as Eve was born from the side of Adam, the church comes from the side of Christ. She is the Bride.

Over time, beginning with St. Paul's letter to the Ephesians, the church began to see an image of this mystery in the union of husband and wife. Something so natural, marriage, became a way of manifesting to the world the love that Christ had for the church. The *Catechism* states:

> The entire Christian life bears the mark of the spousal love of Christ and the Church. Already Baptism, the entry into the People of God, is a nuptial mystery; it is so to speak the nuptial bath which precedes the wedding feast, the Eucharist. Christian marriage in its turn becomes an efficacious sign, the sacrament of the covenant of Christ and the Church. Since it signifies and communicates grace, marriage between baptized persons is a true sacrament of the New Covenant. (CCC 1617)

When a couple is married, they become a living sign for the entire world of the union of Christ and the church.

Thus, the heart of the sacrament of marriage is the moment of consent. The couple, using the words of the church, pledges to be together as long as they both shall live. Human love, of course, wants to last forever. Who professes love for but a moment? In this pledge of love, the couple receives a new grace, a new outpouring of the Spirit that transforms their "natural" commitment into something "supernatural." They become, in this pledge of love, a sign of Christ and the church. Fidelity is thus no longer a matter of spending the rest of their lives with one another. When a couple is faithful to one another, "until death do us part," they live out God's own fidelity to the human family.

Undoubtedly, catechumens may struggle with the church's teaching on the impossibility of divorce in marriage. The church is not "against" divorce like a Republican or Democrat is against a particular tax proposal. Instead, the church recognizes that the Spirit descends in marriage and joins the husband and wife in a conjugal bond, which cannot be ripped apart. The bond is Christ's own love—it is a divine love that is faithful to the end.

Openness to life is also part of the church's teaching because of the bond of love that has united husband and wife. The church doesn't just want couples to have lots of children to control the sex lives of Christians. Instead, the church recognizes that marriage and procreation have always been linked to one another. It's good for children to be raised in a home surrounded by love. Having children is only natural. But in the sacramental gift of marriage, the couple's fertility also becomes part of the sign of Christ's love for the church. Just as the church brings forth children into the world through baptism, the couple brings forth new life through procreation.

Approaching Christian marriage through studying the sacramental nature of marriage may allow for a way of seeing the wisdom of church teaching relative to marriage and family life. It's imprudent, with catechumens, to begin with ethics. Instead, one should begin with the highest ideal. In marriage, everything about love is consecrated to God—doing laundry, having sex, raising a family, paying bills, cleaning up vomit in the middle of night, and caring for ill parents. The liturgy of marriage, in some sense, never ends but is extended to the life of the couple.

The best way to teach this is through having catechists and sponsors who live out the nuptial vocation. RCIA teams should include married couples with kids, who can point to the way that everything, even the mundane, can be transfigured in Christ. Teaching marriage, within the RCIA, thus becomes a way of underlining the surprising gift of Christian initiation. Our communion with God and neighbor unfolds in the everyday.

Those catechumens who are already married will find this teaching on marriage particularly attractive. They'll come to see the ways that the sacramental life of the church has already infused their homes, their love for their spouse. But they may also begin to see ways that they need conversion in their vocation as husband and wife, as father or mother. Sponsors have an important role here in offering spiritual wisdom about nuptial and family life.

In addition to the sacrament of marriage, which sanctifies day-to-day life, there is also the sacrament of holy orders. In the context of the catechumenate, one need not spend too much time on this sacrament. This is not because the sacrament of holy orders is not essential to the salvation of the church. It is! But if too much time is devoted to the sacrament, catechumens may move past a desire for baptism, dreaming instead of being "ordained" as a priest. For some catechumens, this may be their vocation, but one that must be grounded first in their baptismal priesthood.

It's most important to treat this sacrament as linked to baptism. The *Catechism* clarifies:

> The ministerial or hierarchical priesthood of bishops and priests, and the common priesthood of all the faithful participate, "each in its own proper way, in the one priesthood of Christ." While being "ordered one to another," they differ essentially. . . . While the common priesthood of the faithful is exercised by the unfolding of baptismal grace—a life of faith, hope, and charity, a life according to the Spirit—the ministerial priesthood is at the service of the common priesthood. It is directed at the unfolding of the baptismal grace of all Christians. The ministerial priesthood is a means by which Christ unceasingly builds up and leads his Church. For this reason it is transmitted by its own sacrament, the sacrament of Holy Orders. (CCC 1547)

The sacrament of baptism that the catechumen will receive is itself a kind of "ordination" to the baptismal priesthood. As baptismal priests, we are called to make the entirety of our lives an offering to the living God. The ministerial life is essential to this, and there are some men who have been "ordered" to carrying out this task. They have been ordained to act in the person of Christ, to celebrate the sacraments, and to govern the church for the sanctification of the faithful.

Ordination, then, is not about earning some new power. It's not the creation of a superior Christian. Rather, in the sacrament of holy orders, a man is configured more radically to the priesthood of Jesus Christ. He gives his life over to Jesus Christ, his identity is transformed, so that he can teach the Gospel, govern the church, and serve as the sacramental minister of Christ.

Here, we have an occasion to point the catechumens toward a difference between the church and other organizations. Leadership in the church is not earned. It comes as a gift from Christ. The bishop, priest, and deacon should be in awe of their office because they have been chosen to serve as a sign of Christ. Ordination is not a right but an unmerited gift coming from the church.

Undoubtedly, some catechumens will wonder why men alone can receive the gift of ordination. If the sacrament is presented as a "special gift given only to certain men," there will be no way to answer this challenge. Instead, the way to address this question is to highlight the dignity of the baptismal priesthood. The ministerial priesthood is not better than the baptismal priesthood. They're different. Men and women are called to sanctify the created order, and the ministerial priesthood is at the service of this priesthood. The priest acts in the person of Christ, becoming a sign of Jesus. His "maleness" is not unimportant to the sacrament. But he did not receive this sacrament because he was male. He received it so that he could configure himself even more closely to Christ, to give his whole self over to the salvation of the People of God. If the sacrament becomes about power or prestige, something is wrong.

Catechumens should be invited to attend an ordination of a deacon, priest, or bishop. The liturgy conveys more about the ministerial priesthood than anything else. Likewise, the catechumens learn the most about the priesthood by spending time with priests, who can share a bit about their vocation.

Marriage and ordination can often be sticky subjects to teach catechumens. But we have to understand the way that these sacraments are ordered toward the cultivation of communion. They're not about power, prestige, or denying people's freedom. Like all the sacraments, they're about the consecration of love to the living God.

Lastly, in both cases, it should be underlined that neither marriage nor ordination are necessary for Christian salvation. Many people are not married. Most are not ordained. Some Christians become consecrated religious. Others live the single life, sharing their baptismal vocation with friends and society as a whole. The sacraments at the service of communion are ways of sanctifying concrete states or forms of life. But the fundamental sacraments of consecration, of Christian vocation, remain baptism, confirmation, and regular participation in the Eucharist.

The Liturgical Formation of Candidates for Full Communion

Thus far, I have said nothing specific about the liturgical formation of those seeking to be received into the full communion of the Catholic Church. This omission has been intentional. Even those who have been involved in the RCIA for years are often unaware that the RCIA is not intended for Christians entering into the full communion of the Catholic Church.

At present, there are possibilities for combined rites in which baptized Christians are placed alongside catechumens. There is a combined rite celebrating the acceptance of catechumens and those seeking full communion. At the Rite of Election, one may also include a call to continuing conversion of the candidates for full communion. Most dioceses will use these rites.

But these rites are not necessary. Reception into full communion, unlike the RCIA, is not oriented to the reception of sacraments

during the Easter season. One may be received into full communion at any point in the liturgical year. The University of Notre
Dame, for example, receives Christians into full communion at
multiple times during the year. It is not appropriate to receive
candidates for full communion at the Easter Vigil. These rites are
intended for those seeking full initiation—baptism, confirmation,
and Eucharist as adults—into the Catholic Church.

Preparation for reception into full communion is oriented
toward forming the Christian as an ecclesial person within the
Roman Catholic communion:

> The baptized Christian is to receive both doctrinal and spiritual
> preparation, adapted to individual pastoral requirements, for re-
> ception into the full communion of the Catholic Church. The can-
> didate should learn to deepen an inner adherence to the Church,
> where he or she will find the fullness of his or her baptism. . . .
> Anything that would equate candidates for reception with those
> who are catechumens is to be absolutely avoided. (RCIA 477)

For this reason, the candidates should never be dismissed from
Mass because they are baptized. They should never be anointed
as if they are catechumens. They are not catechumens. They are
candidates, already baptized into the love of the Father, the Son,
and the Holy Spirit.

Candidates for full communion will come to their local parish
with a variety of experiences. Some may be from evangelical tradi-
tions, with informal liturgies, emphasizing preaching. They may
know a good deal about the Scriptures, but they may be suspicious of some of the liturgical practices of Catholics. Others may
be members of mainline Protestant communities, with liturgical
rites similar to Catholics. They may have questions or concerns
about some of the sacraments such as marriage, Marian devotion,
and a Catholic understanding of eucharistic sacrifice. Others will
have received their baptism as children, having never celebrated
the sacraments of confirmation or received communion. They're
technically baptized but may look more like a catechumen, com-

pletely unaware of Scripture, Catholic teaching, or what it means to belong to a church. Even these last Christians have been baptized, and it is inappropriate to form them in Catholic life in a way that makes them seem equivalent to catechumens.

It is my recommendation that reception for full communion be conducted entirely apart from preparing catechumens for baptism. This separate process includes their formation into the liturgical-sacramental life of the church. This process of formation will include three dimensions.

First, an initial series of conversations should take place with a pastor, catechist, or other mature parishioner. The purpose of this conversation is to listen to the history, the story, of the candidate for full communion. Why are they interested in joining the Catholic Church? What is their experience of worshiping in a community of faith? What questions do they have about the church? What are they concerned about? A series of honest conversations will establish the individualized curriculum for each candidate.

Second, the candidate for full communion should participate in the robust adult faith formation that is part of parish life. This could mean attending celebrations of the Word of God with catechumens, since some of these celebrations could be open to the entire parish. But they should spend time with adults who are studying the *Catechism*, praying with the Bible, feeding the hungry and clothing the naked, singing in the choir, praying the Liturgy of the Hours, receiving spiritual formation for the sacrament of marriage, and setting up chairs for the parish festival.

For those who are already baptized, the United States bishops have said:

> Their doctrinal and spiritual preparation for reception into full Catholic communion should be determined according to the individual case, that is, it should depend on the extent to which the baptized person has led a Christian life within a community of faith and been appropriately catechized to deepen his or her inner adherence to the Church. (National Statutes for the Catechumenate, 30)

For those baptized Christians who have been living a Christian life, their preparation could be very brief. For those with no experience with Christian life, there should be a lengthy process of adult faith formation similar to that of the catechumens. In addition, serious one-on-one conversations with catechists and clergy should be held throughout their period of formation.

During this period of time, there will be a need to explain in particular the sacrament of confirmation, the Eucharist, and penance. Candidates for full communion should celebrate the sacrament of penance before the rite of reception. They should have a sense about the apostolic nature of confirmation. They should see the Eucharist as a sacrament of love, longing to participate regularly in the Supper of the Lamb. If married, they should see the sacramental power of their own nuptial union, the way that they are called to manifest to the world the union of Christ and the church. They don't need to know everything about the sacraments or the liturgy. But they do need to know how to adore the living God and long to be sanctified through the rites of the church.

Third, the parish should celebrate the rite of reception into full communion as often as it is necessary to do so. For some parishes, this could be only once a year. Others could celebrate it five times a year. Some entering into formation for full communion may need to wait a year or so to prepare for entry into the church. Others may be ready after a couple of weeks. Candidates for full communion should be received into full communion, receiving the sacrament of confirmation and their first Communion, at a parish Sunday Mass as soon as they are ready.

One major objection to this proposal is that many parishes would have no moment of initiation to celebrate during the Easter Vigil without these receptions into full communion. My parish in Boston, for example, had only two adult baptisms during my four years in the parish. The Easter Vigil, however, is *not* simply a celebration of the initiation of new members. Instead, it is the celebration of the church who waits with longing outside the tomb of the risen Lord. There is joy in this celebration whether or not new members are being initiated. But it's not bad to experience a bit of sadness that there is no one to baptize, for such sadness could elicit in parishes a responsibility for the work of evangelization. In the coming years, with the decline in infant baptisms, there will be more adults to baptize. If a parish hasn't had an adult baptism in a while, it may be time to more intentionally proclaim the Good News that Jesus Christ is Lord. After all, that's what the renewal of our baptismal promises at the Easter Vigil is about too!

Thus, the appropriate way to form the liturgical and sacramental imagination of candidates for full communion is the everyday context of parish life. This means that the liturgical life of a church is *actually* formative, an encounter with Jesus Christ rather than a dull, deadening experience of mumbling, out-of-tune priests, lectors, and choirs.

Conclusion

During their formation, we are to offer catechumens and candidates a liturgical hypothesis. This hypothesis does not simply involve teaching them about the liturgy and the sacraments. Instead, we must show how every dimension of our lives can become an offering of praise to the living God. We must show how the rites of the church offer to us mere mortals a way of becoming divine. The rest of Christian life, as it turns out, is nothing but a verification of this hypothesis.

Chapter 3

Liturgical Formation in the Period of Purification and Enlightenment

Before college, I never exercised. My freshman year of high school had been my last year of physical education. When I arrived on campus as an undergraduate, I was overweight and unhealthy. I ate what I wanted, slept as much as I wanted, and rarely broke a sweat except when suffering from the flu.

My sophomore year, I decided to change. My roommates all went to the gym regularly, and they told me it would be good for me to exercise. To be honest, I didn't know where to start. So, my friend John accompanied me to the gym and told me how to use some of the machines. Soon, I was going to the gym three or four times per week. I cut out drinking Coke and eating beef with every meal. I began to lose weight.

More important, I learned to love exercise. I went for long walks. I began running, biking, swimming, and lifting weights. I loved exercising and found that it helped me sleep better, think better, and feel better.

Summer came, and I was hooked. I no longer saw my friends every day but spent an hour at the gym. I began to walk five miles a day. My friends had provided me a hypothesis that I needed to hear: it's time for you to exercise, and it will make you happier. They were right! But I had to verify their hypothesis, live it out. I had to make exercise a habit. I had to become a person who exercises.

This process of verification transformed my life. Even today, eighteen years since that first proposal, I spend a portion of each day exercising. If two or three days pass without a long walk or a trip to the gym, I feel like something is wrong. At this point, my whole body knows that exercise is good, healthy, and part of a happy life.

Verification in the Period of Purification and Enlightenment

During the catechumenate, we have proposed a fundamental, life-altering hypothesis to the catechumen: human beings are made for divine worship, for the art of self-giving love made possible through relationship with Jesus Christ. We have clarified our hypothesis through reference to the whole teaching of the church, as well as embodying it through experiences of common worship. We have shown how every dimension of the moral life, our love of those on the margins, is intrinsic to the activity of Christian worship.

But there comes a time for the catechumens to verify this hypothesis, to write it on their very body. One can think about the period of purification and enlightenment as a moment of verification. The catechumens join with the whole Christian community in "becoming a living sacrifice" to God. As the RCIA states:

> The period of purification and enlightenment, which the rite of election begins, customarily coincides with Lent. In the liturgy and liturgical catechesis of Lent the reminder of baptism already received or the preparation for its reception, as well as the theme of repentance, renew the entire community along with those being prepared to celebrate the paschal mystery, in which each of the elect will share through the sacraments of initiation. For both the elect and the local community, therefore, the Lenten season is a time for spiritual recollection in preparation for the celebration of the paschal mystery. (RCIA 138)

The period of purification and enlightenment is intrinsically tied to the liturgical season of Lent. Lent is not simply a forty-day period in which Christians contemplate the sacrifice of Christ on the cross. In the Office of Readings in the Roman Rite during the first weeks of Lent, we read from the book of Exodus. We enter with Israel into the desert, letting God reform our hearts to properly worship the living God. During Lent, we fast so that we may hunger for God alone. We pray so that all our attention may be directed to God. We give alms in offering our money to the hungry and the thirsty, and we recognize that everything we have is first and foremost a gift from God.

The season of Lent is that period of time in which Christians verify through their very bodies the ultimate hypothesis—we are made for worship. We were created to desire God alone. The period of purification and enlightenment is set aside for the task of forming not just the elect but every one of us in divine desire (RCIA 139).

This period of the RCIA is not intended for offering more catechetical instruction. Because so many parishes forget that the catechumenate may last longer than a year, we often forget about this norm. We squeeze as much instruction in as possible, transitioning quickly from the Rite of Election to lectures on eschatology, the church, and the communion of saints. Everything that we have not been able to cover in the Creed thus far, we take up during this period of formation.

Lent is not the time for such explicit instruction of the catechumens. It is the time to enter with the elect into the desert, to walk with them as they prepare to become sons and daughters of the living God through baptism, confirmation, and the Eucharist. For this reason, the rites appropriate to this period are the essential "content" of spiritual formation.

Enrollment as the Doorway to Verification

The period of purification and enlightenment commences with the Rite of Election. This rite, celebrated at the beginning of Lent in a diocese, is "called election because the acceptance made by the Church is founded on the election by God, in whose name the Church acts" (RCIA 119). The pivotal moment of the rite is the enrollment of names, in which the catechumens pledge their fidelity to receive the sacraments of initiation during the Easter Vigil. The bishop celebrates the Rite of Election ideally within the cathedral, since the bishop on his *cathedra*, or chair, serves as a living sign of the church. Before the rite, godparents are chosen.

The Rite of Election should be celebrated during Mass on the First Sunday of Lent. The gospel text during the First Sunday of Lent is always the temptation of Jesus in the desert. The homily for the Rite of Election focuses the catechumens once more on the ultimate hypothesis proposed during the catechumenate—we are made for worship. Jesus enters into the desert, into the wilderness, for two reasons. He enters into the wilderness, the chaos, of the human condition—the space where hunger, thirst, and the quest for power are all too obvious to us. He also goes into the wilderness because the desert is the trysting place of God with Israel. There, Jesus is tempted by the devil to seize power and control like Adam rather than be the beloved Son of the Father, who is made for love unto the end. Jesus demonstrates to us that entrance into the desert will not mean leaving behind our humanity, but learning to rely on God with the fullness of our being. We enter with Jesus into the desert so that we too can become a worshipful being, offering our whole selves to God in love. For this is precisely what Jesus accomplished on the cross, love unto the end.

The homily is immediately followed by the presentation of the candidates. The rite dictates that each of the catechumens is called by name. Thus far, the hypothesis of worshipful wisdom and divine blessing has been offered to the catechumens as a group. They have been able to see themselves as part of the "RCIA group of St. Patrick's parish." But no more! Each catechumen is called by name. He or she is asked to verify the hypothesis with their whole being, as Mary or John, Carlos or Juanita.

The celebrant then asks the godparents to testify to the veracity of the catechumens' desire. Yes, it is time for the catechumens to verify with their whole lives their commitment to Jesus Christ. But even here, they are not alone. The godparents function as sacramental signs of the whole church, who have walked with them through the catechumenate. The godparents "verify" the catechumens' desire for verification; they are best friends of the new friends of Jesus.

The catechumens then are called to proclaim their desire to belong to the elect, to receive the sacraments of initiation at Easter. The presider addresses them, asking that they commit themselves to respond to the call that they have heard: "do you wish to enter fully into the life of the Church through the sacraments of baptism, confirmation, and the eucharist?" (RCIA 132).

Thus far, the catechumens have expressed this desire through the contingency of speech. They have proclaimed their "I do" with vigor. But as we know, speech quickly fades away. We've all proclaimed at least once in our lives, "I love you," wanting it to last forever. But we discovered months later that our profession of love was not eternal. For, we learned that we did not love this person forever.

The act of enrolling names, of writing one's names in a book, is different. Writing is permanent. What had remained perhaps a vague wish, a hope, is now written. It's there for all to see. The names of those baptized Christians who have preceded these catechumens are there too. Baptism, of course, is the moment of initiation into the fullness of the church. But in this act of enrollment, the catechumen experiences a foretaste of belonging fully to the church. The bishop responds to this commitment—this fidelity to Christ and the church—by admitting the catechumens to the elect.

The act of enrolling names is a remarkable moment for the life of a blossoming Christian. It is a sacramental moment in the life of a person, who no longer hopes to become a Christian but pledges through the grace of the Spirit to do so. The remainder of the period of purification and enlightenment is an occasion to prepare to do so, to desire with all of one's heart to enter into communion with God.

The Scrutinies as Verifying Election

On the Third, Fourth, and Fifth Sundays of Lent, the church celebrates the scrutinies. The purpose of the scrutinies is to "uncover, then heal all that is weak, defective, or sinful in the hearts of the elect; to bring out, then strengthen all that is upright, strong, and good" (RCIA 141). The celebration of the scrutinies includes listening to the Sunday gospel (the woman at the well, the man born blind, and the raising of Lazarus), a homily, silent prayer, intercessions, an exorcism, a hymn, and the elect's dismissal.

For many Americans, the scrutinies may appear as excessive. They focus on the sinfulness of the elect, at times praying to God that the elect would recognize themselves as sinners. The elect are asked to stand before the assembly, if possible, kneeling before God as a sign of their penitence.

Yet, if the elect have been well formed in the sacrament of penance, they know what they're doing. Conversion in the Christian life is related to love. The gospel readings during the Third, Fourth, and Fifth Sundays of Lent (Year A) pertain to God's commitment of love, and they shape the elect to respond to this love with a total gift of self.

On the Third Sunday of Lent, we contemplate Jesus's encounter with the Samaritan woman at the well. Jesus does not meet the woman at any well, but at Jacob's well, the very place that Jacob first kissed his wife-to-be Rebecca. In his encounter with this woman, Jesus teaches her about the living water of baptism that will lead to eternal life. But he does so as the Bridegroom. After all, the first sign that Jesus did in the Gospel of John was to transform water into wine. Providing wine was the responsibility of the Bridegroom, and Jesus is indeed that one! He has come to marry not only Israel but the Samaritans too, announcing himself as the source of living water.

Yes, the Samaritan woman has sinned, having more than one husband. But notice that her name is never used. That's because we're supposed to see ourselves as the Samaritan woman, meeting Jesus Christ the Bridegroom at the noonday well. Baptism is a nuptial sacrament where we experience a new level of intimacy with Jesus Christ. The exorcism this day is not just about how badly we have sinned. Instead, the exorcism prepares the whole assembly, including the elect, to desire God *totally*.

On the Fourth Sunday of Lent, we turn to the man born blind. In the Gospel of John, few actually understand who Jesus is. The disciples, the Pharisees, and the crowds all mistake Jesus for some wonder worker, unable to see him as the Word made flesh. But not the man born blind. Despite his inability to see at the beginning, through Jesus's healing, he alone comes to recognize who Jesus is. The man born blind confesses belief in the Lord and worships him.

There is an obvious interpretation of this reading, often given by homilists. In fact, this interpretation is found in the rite itself. The man is born blind, abiding in the darkness of sin. Through his encounter with Jesus Christ, he receives his sight and thus is able to worship the living God.

But the gospel doesn't entirely support this reading. After all, the blindness of the man is not caused by his sin or the sin of his parents. Jesus Christ enters into his suffering and heals him. He bestows light. And the man receives this gift of life, a donation of love by Jesus, offering himself in return through the act of worship.

This scrutiny thus provides an occasion for the elect and the entire assembly to question whether we have responded to the gift of Christ's light with worshipful love. Have we imitated the man born blind, offering ourselves to Jesus, or do we walk around like those in the dark, unable to see who our Lord is? The blessing over the elect at the end of the second scrutiny reminds us not just to learn from Jesus but also to worship him through word and witness: "Let them rejoice in your light, that they may see, and, like the man born blind whose sight you restored, let them prove to be staunch and fearless witnesses to the faith" (RCIA 168A).

On the Fifth Sunday of Lent, we celebrate the third and final scrutiny. The gospel for this Sunday is the dramatic raising of Lazarus from the dead, functioning in John's gospel as the last sign pointing toward Jesus's own resurrection. Once again, the gospel contains ample possibilities to speak about Christ's love. When Jesus learns that Lazarus is dead, he cries. He comes out of love for Martha, Mary, and Lazarus to raise him from the dead. But he also comes so that all may see this sign and believe.

The image of death will be one that the elect are familiar with. Death, like sin, cuts us off from communion. It's the great problem that every human being has to deal with—what is the meaning of a life in which death is inevitable? A life that is contingent? Christ comes to rescue us in our contingency, to heal us from the darkness of sin and death alike. The raising of Lazarus provides a foretaste of hope. We will celebrate the resurrection of Jesus Christ at Easter, and we ourselves are destined to be raised from the dead.

And the elect will also be raised from the dead through the sacraments of baptism, confirmation, and the Eucharist. They will enter into new life with God, a communion that relativizes death. Yes, we will still die. But we die in Christ, aware that death does not have the last word.

The elect are to enter the tomb with Lazarus, just as the entire church prepares to commemorate the death and resurrection of Jesus Christ. Christ is coming to marry us, to heal us, to raise us from the dead. All that's left to do is to long for it with all of one's being.

The Presentation of the Creed and the Lord's Prayer

During the period of enlightenment and purification, the elect receive both the Creed and the Lord's Prayer. The Creed is presented to the elect after the first scrutiny. The rite, which should be celebrated in the context of the community of the faithful, includes readings, a homily, the recitations of the Apostles' or Nicene Creed by celebrant and assembly, and a prayer over the elect. The Lord's Prayer is presented to the elect after the third scrutiny. The rite, also celebrated with the faithful, includes readings, a gospel proclamation from Matthew of the Lord's Prayer, a homily, a prayer over the elect, and their dismissal.

These rites were practiced in the early church during a time in which many would have never heard the Creed or Lord's Prayer before these moments. But what do these rites mean in a world in which one can Google the words of these prayers? The elect, by hearing the Creed proclaimed by the assembly, by listening to the Lord's Prayer, are invited to write it on their hearts. They're invited to memorize these texts. Memorization is a forgotten aspect of Christian formation. When we memorize something, it becomes part of us. It's "mine." That's why we spend so much time teaching little kids the Pledge of Allegiance in school—we want them to think of themselves, for good or for ill, as Americans.

For us Christians, the Creed and the Lord's Prayer are a summary of the whole Gospel, the entire mystery of love revealed in Christ. To memorize these prayers is a radical act of acceptance by the elect. It means that the elect have made the Gospel their own, allowing it to be written on their hearts. It is an act of verification.

On Holy Saturday, there is a Rite of Recitation of the Creed. This rite includes readings from the Scriptures, a prayer, the recitation of the Creed by the elect, and the ephphetha rite. The ephphetha rite is named for the moment of Jesus's healing when he opens the ears of a man born without hearing. Right before the elect receive the sacraments of initiation, the celebrant touches their ears and closed mouths and prays that the elect may profess the faith that they have heard.

By now, the elect have heard so much. They have heard, perhaps for years, about the mystery of love revealed in Christ. And now, a new vocation is given to them. They will not just "hear" about this mystery of faith; it's time to proclaim it. It's time to let all of one's senses be informed by this mystery of faith. It's time to stand before the holy church of God and say, "I believe in God, the Father almighty . . . " And in saying this, they pledge themselves to this mystery of faith.

This rite is a fitting *inclusio* to their time of Christian formation. In the catechumenate, they had the cross traced over each of their senses. Now, as they are about to enter into the waters of salvation, their senses are once more blessed. And soon, on that most dazzling of nights, their whole bodies will be consecrated to the triune God.

Easter Vigil as Verification

The culmination of the entire Triduum is the Easter Vigil. The liturgy for the Vigil has four parts: the solemn blessing of the paschal candle, a lengthy cursus of the Scriptures recalling what

God has accomplished in Christ, baptism and confirmation, and finally the celebration of the Eucharist. These four parts of the Vigil are essential to the final formation of the elect, shaping their very bodies into temples where the living God may dwell.

The Vigil begins in the dark, outside the church. Here, perhaps years before, the catechumens were greeted by the celebrant as they began their journey. And now they stand as the elect at the entry of the church in total dark except for the presence of a glowing fire. The fire, like everything on this night, is to be blessed:

> O God, who through your Son
> bestowed upon the faithful the fire of your glory,
> sanctify this new fire, we pray,
> and grant that,
> by these paschal celebrations,
> we may be so inflamed with heavenly desires,
> that with minds made pure
> we may attain festivities of unending splendor. (*Roman Missal*,
> The Blessing of the Fire and Preparation of the Candle, 10)

The blessing of this fire introduces once more the sacramental principle at the heart of Catholic life. The God who used matter to reveal himself will *on this night* transform matter once more. The Vigil that we celebrate is about assuming a posture of desire, letting the candles that we hold transform our very hearts. We should long for God ardently just like this candle burns with heat.

The candle is then marked with the year and consecrated with burning incense. The cross on the candle transforms this wax into a living sign of Christ's presence. The five grains of incense are images of his wounds that now make possible the redemption of all humanity—especially, on this night, the elect.

The lit candle enters the dark church. After the Mass of the Lord's Supper, the church building has dwelt in near total darkness, except for the presence of sunlight. The candle in front of the tabernacle has been extinguished as the light of the world, Jesus Christ, had been snuffed out through sin. But even in the midst of total suffering, of the worst horrors that human beings can inflict on the Word made flesh, love wins. Light shines. For the elect, they inevitably recognize this truth. Often, over the last year(s), their godparents and catechists have taught them to see how the light of love has shone even in the midst of the darkness. And now, *on this night*, the light shines once more.

The singing of the *Exsultet*, which is the formal, almost eucharistic, blessing of this candle, invites the whole assembly to assume a posture of expectation. The Vigil on this night is not about lamenting the death of the Word made flesh. It is a hopeful vigil as the church gathers to "Rejoice, let Mother Church also rejoice, arrayed with the lightning of his glory."

This entire night, through the work of Jesus Christ as mediated through this candle, has been consecrated to God. The *Exsultet* repeats the refrain, "This is the night." For on this night, Israel was rescued from slavery, Israel was led through the darkness of the desert, and now Christ rose from the dead. Because of God's involvement in history, this night—and every subsequent night—is marked by the power of a dazzling, divine love. Such love has the power to consecrate this candle, to transform it into a sacrificial offering to God, mingling "with the lights of heaven." So too, the gathering assembly is to become this offering to God. It is our whole bodies, infused with desire for God, that is part of this offering.

The great Vigil begins as the assembly sits to listen to the Word of God. And what a feast of readings! On the mother of all vigils, the church provides nine readings (seven from the Old Testament, two from the New Testament). Ideally, all should be read. The lengthy readings from the Old Testament reveal God's divine pedagogy, the salvation of the world beginning with the creation of the world, the sacrifice of Isaac, the crossing of the Red Sea, the promise of the New Jerusalem in the Prophets, the gift of wisdom, and the resurrection of the body as a temple of the living God. The *Gloria* is then sung, followed by a reading from Saint Paul and the gospel of the resurrection.

For the elect, in particular, this is an occasion to consider once more the wondrous works that God has accomplished in history. God has acted in the past not in a willy-nilly way but with wisdom—an ordering principle that can make sense of all of history. This principle, as it turns out, is love unto the end. The power of divine love is stronger than even death. When Jesus Christ is raised from the dead, his human body is transformed. And now, we wait. We wait because we know that our risen Lord still acts. He still transforms matter, transfigures history, into a place of love.

The baptismal liturgy performs for the whole church this transfiguration of history. The God who created the world in love, who entered into a covenant with Israel, who redeemed all of us in Christ, now acts *this night* through these *elect*. The elect are called forward to the front of the church with their godparents. They process to the baptismal font accompanied by the singing of the Litany of the Saints. This litany asks that the whole company of men and women will pray for us this night, as they always do, of course. The litany underlines that the baptisms that are to be carried out this night are not just the concern of this parish church. The elect are preparing to enter into the whole communion of believers, the living and the dead, who long for them to participate in so glorious a communion.

Following the litany, the baptismal waters are blessed. This blessing prayer, for the elect, should already be quite familiar in their study of baptism. They hear in this prayer, the wonders of a God who breathed over the waters at creation in love, who flooded creation, redeeming it from sin, who brought Israel into the Promised Land through the Red Sea, who was baptized by John in the Jordan River, and from whom blood and water came forth on the cross. *This* God acts on *this* night, transforming the created waters into the space of divine salvation:

> May this water receive by the Holy Spirit
> the grace of your Only Begotten Son,
> so that human nature, created in your image
> and washed clean through the Sacrament of Baptism
> from all the squalor of the life of old,
> may be found worthy to rise to the life of newborn children
> through water and the Holy Spirit.
> (*Roman Missal*, Blessing of Baptismal Water)

In baptism, the elect will not simply receive a bath. They will enter into the waters where Jesus Christ himself dwells, where love is present, and will die to sin and death. They will die to a false understanding of our vocation as consumers and producers and rise as those made to adore the living God. Their stories now have a new trajectory, made possible through Christ's resurrection from the dead.

After the blessing, the elect then profess the Creed. They have heard this night about the mystery of love, and now they profess their faith that this story alone is the true one. They say this night that Satan has no power. He is nothing. The powers of darkness are meaningless, for love alone is credible.

And then the elect are lowered into the baptismal waters. Ideally, this baptism should be performed through immersion since it performs the radical change that baptism makes possible. We're not just talking about a little change of identity, a little cleansing, with just a bit of water. The change is total. The new Christian is baptized in the name of the Father, the Son, and the Holy Spirit. They have professed faith in this God through the Creed, but now they verify this profession with their very bodies. Their identity is now intimately and absolutely tied to a God who is total and absolute love.

This transformation of identity is made manifest through the gift of a lit candle and the wearing of a white garment. The neophytes are the ones who have been enlightened through Christ; they have put on a garment of salvation. And at this moment, they once more manifest to the assembly the wondrous gift we have received. Baptism is not just about belonging to a local parish or a group of people. It's a transformation of my whole self in Christ. That's why on this night, even if there aren't baptisms and confirmations, we still renew our baptismal promises. The neophytes accomplish their new ministry among us through processing to the front of the assembly, while the following antiphon is sung: "I saw water flowing from the Temple, from its right-hand side, alleluia; and all to whom this water came were saved and shall say: Alleluia, alleluia." Indeed, we have seen this water flowing out of the side of Jesus Christ on the cross, and we have now seen it once more in that baptismal font where men and women enter into a new relationship with the God who is love.

After baptism, confirmation is celebrated. On this night, unless the bishop is present and confers baptism, the priest is the celebrant for confirmation. The neophytes have entered into Christ's very life, and through the reception of confirmation, they are more fully conformed to the image of the Son. The celebrant stretches his hands out over those to be confirmed and asks that the Holy Spirit descend on these sons and daughters, that they may be given the full gift of the Spirit. They also receive an anointing with chrism, transforming them into a fragrant offering to God.

Only now does the entire assembly renew its baptismal vows. Often, the renewal of baptismal promises is done as a way of filling time between the clothing of the neophytes with the baptismal garment and confirmation. But this misses out on a formative opportunity for the assembly and neophytes alike. Those recently baptized and confirmed would see the renewal of the baptismal promises by the assembly. They would recognize the faces of their godparents, their catechists, those they have grown to love as brothers and sisters in Christ. Through baptism, they have become part of this assembly.

Now, the neophytes join the assembly to offer the eucharistic prayer for the first time. Their bodies have been consecrated to God through water and oil. And at last, after being dismissed for the duration of the catechumenate, they pray the eucharistic prayer. They smell the glorious incense, and they process forward to eat and drink the living God.

Participating in the eucharistic banquet was the purpose of their entire initiation. This was it! As those made to adore the living God, to commune with the Word made flesh, they now at last enjoy this communion in the midst of the church. We have proposed to them, over the years, that they are made to adore the living God. They have been made for worship. And now, at last, the neophytes can exercise their vocation in the presence of the assembly.

And the wonder of the Eucharist is that they can celebrate this sacrament for the rest of their days. Each time they assemble in the church, they are invited to sup at the eucharistic altar. The Eucharist is that sacrament of initiation that is never finished insofar as each time we eat and drink his Body and Blood, we once more exercise our vocation as worshipers of the once dead and now risen Lord.

Conclusion

The RCIA, as we've seen, is a pilgrimage. The seeker comes into the church, provoked to ask, "What is here?" They stay a bit and perhaps discover that in this space is the presence of the living God. They begin to change, to experience conversion, and they become through the Rite of Acceptance catechumens. During this time, the church proposes the hypothesis that human beings are made for love, for worship of the triune God. The catechumen begins to practice, to live out this hypothesis in day-to-day life. As Lent begins, the catechumen becomes part of the elect. They prepare to give their whole bodies over to Christ, verifying the truth of the Gospel with their whole selves. And finally, on the night that defines all nights, they perform the ultimate act of verification. They enter into the waters of salvation, they receive an outpouring of the Spirit, and they sup at the banquet of the Lamb once slain.

The rest of their Christian lives, if these lives last a week or ninety years, are reflections on the wondrous gift they have received in Jesus Christ. It is the lengthy, permanent, and perpetual process of mystagogy.

Chapter 4

Liturgical Formation as Mystagogy

I looked down at the gold shimmering on my left hand. After years of waiting, I had finally married Kara. On that Monday morning, following a whirlwind weekend, the ring was a tangible sign of the transformation that took place at the Basilica of the Sacred Heart on that snow-globe-like December day. As I carried out day-to-day tasks like typing on a computer, opening a door, and taking notes in class, I was acutely aware of the presence of the ring and thus of the reality of my spouse. The reality that I was the husband to her!

Of course, time passed. Over the last decade, the ring, while still gold, is now marked with scratches. The ring has conformed my hand to its shape. I no longer notice its presence while engaging in most activities, since the ring has become almost part of my hand.

Yet the ring still functions as a sign of that deep mystery of love that has become the defining event of my life. The scratches invite me to recognize the wounds of love, the manner in which self-gift across time and space changes who we are. The ring has conformed my finger to itself, a visible sign that this mystery of love has marked my very body.

In this sense, the ring that I wear is not reducible to a shiny piece of gold. It is the tangible, visible sign of a mystery. Sure, there may be more valuable pieces of gold in the world. But this ring is a sign of a love lived well yesterday, today, and—God-willing—for years to come.

The Period of Mystagogy

Everyone who has worked with the RCIA knows that the period of mystagogy, following initiation, is the least developed in the church. Many RCIA groups, for example, tend to treat this period as an optional one. The first meeting after the Easter Vigil will involve a bit of reflection on the liturgies associated with initiation. Then, the parish if time allows will introduce the neophytes to stewardship (time, talent, and treasure), signing up for ministry in the church, themes related to Christian vocation, and will conclude with some sort of meal as a community. If Easter is early, this period will often be the time to cover material from the *Catechism* that couldn't be treated during the catechumenate. If Easter is late, the period might be only a couple of weeks before school lets out for the summer.

The approach that most parishes take to mystagogy is insufficient. The purpose of this period, according to the RCIA, is to set aside "a time for the community and the neophytes together to grow in deepening their grasp of the paschal mystery and in making it part of their lives through meditation on the Gospel, sharing in the eucharist, and doing the works of charity" (RCIA 244). The goal of mystagogy isn't to sign up the recently initiated to serve in the roles of communion minister or lector. Rather, mystagogy should be within the context of the entire parish, inviting each member of Christ's Body to discern how Christ's death and resurrection has been transformative of one's whole life. The privileged practices engaged in during mystagogy are the core aspects of Christian living: listening to the Word of God, supping at the eucharistic banquet, and sharing this eucharistic love with those in need. Mystagogy, as the RCIA treats it, is both contemplating and living the mystery of Christ's love in the world.

This doesn't mean that the neophytes should disappear into the broader body of the church now that they are initiated. This too often happens. They still have a vocation among the People of God. Through their experience of having recently tasted the sweetness of eucharistic love, they act as leaven within the assembly, reminding each of us of the gift of Christian life. The neophytes will come to recognize how valuable they are within the community of faith, and the whole body of the faithful will celebrate the mystery of love made present through these men and women.

The privileged location of catechesis during the Easter Season is the Sunday Eucharist. Too often, parishes seem to spend themselves entirely during the Lenten season, with little energy to celebrate the resurrection of Christ. But the Masses during Easter are equally as formative of Christian identity as the Lenten liturgies. From the Second Sunday of Easter on, the neophytes hear of St. Thomas's encounter with the risen Lord; the disciples' meeting with Jesus in the breaking of the bread while on the way to Emmaus; the identification of Jesus as the Good Shepherd who feeds his flock with the finest of foods; Jesus as the true vine who unites us more deeply to God, to himself, and to each other; the command to love one another as Christ loved us. The season culminates in the feasts of the Ascension and Pentecost, where we gaze with wonder on the church as the very flesh of Christ, who makes his presence now among us.

The neophytes should be given a special space in the assembly during these eucharistic liturgies. On the Second Sunday of Easter (also called *Dominica in albis* or Sunday in white), it is appropriate for them to wear their baptismal garment to church. There should be intercessions particular to the neophytes throughout the Easter Season. Pentecost should serve as a special occasion closing this period. Likewise, the neophytes should not forget their baptismal date but should be brought together on the anniversary of their baptism to celebrate a liturgy. During Easter, the bishop should also meet with the neophytes if he did not celebrate their initiation.

Thus, the period of mystagogy is a chance to celebrate the wondrous transformation that has taken place in Christ's Body, the church. Jesus died and has been raised from the dead through the power of the Spirit. The newly initiated are signs of Christ's power working among us, evidence that love still conquers death here and now.

The whole parish is responsible for this mystagogical formation. It's not just the RCIA team but the parish itself that should be immersed in the work of mystagogy during Easter.

Contemplating and Living the Mystery

This chapter opened with a description of the wondrous "sign" of my wedding ring. I don't simply contemplate the mystery of my marriage once a year on my anniversary. Yes, this day is a special occasion to celebrate my marriage—to go out for dinner, to watch our wedding video, or to spend time with our children, the fruit of our union. Yes, the ring is part of my daily life, constantly inviting me to contemplate the mystery of marriage.

So too, mystagogy is not exclusive to the post-Easter season. Yes, there is a time to contemplate the paschal mystery of Jesus Christ through the Easter Season. But, every aspect of Christian life is to be infused with a mystagogical posture. Mystagogy is a stance toward the entirety of life, seeing every part of our existence through the mystery of Christ. This is the purpose of liturgical catechesis, forming us in worshipful wisdom from day to day. As the *Catechism* aptly expresses, "Liturgical catechesis aims to initiate people into the mystery of Christ (It is 'mystagogy.') by proceeding from the visible to the invisible, from the sign to the thing signified, from the 'sacraments' to the 'mysteries'" (CCC 1075).

The neophytes, if the liturgical formation has been robust throughout the catechumenate and period of enlightenment, should already have been initiated into this mystagogical way of the sacramental life of the church. They will have thought through each of the sacraments, each liturgical rite, aware of the way that the rite answers the deepest needs of the human condition. They will have understood how the liturgical prayer of the church enters us into salvation history. They will have learned the proper dispositions to participate fruitfully in this prayer, capable of shaping their whole lives as a worshipful offering to God. A mystagogical posture was integral to the formation laid out in this book.

But the Easter Season provides an opportunity to "recapitulate" or "reiterate" this mystagogical formation. Good educators know that formation is not about learning something and then moving on. The liturgical year is built around a structure in which we return to the same themes again and again, entering more deeply into the Christian mystery throughout the liturgical year. There are specific mystagogical practices, already implicit throughout the catechumenate and period of purification and enlightenment that can lead the neophytes into a more fruitful contemplation and living out of the Christian mystery.

The first dimension of this mystagogy is fruitfully drawing wisdom from what took place at the Easter Vigil. The Vigil is a powerful liturgical event. For this reason, the temptation is to focus on the event itself. It was nice when I was baptized, and everyone was excited. It was good to have the Eucharist for the first time. It was amazing to see the whole parish express such joy!

This basic, human experience is not to be passed over. When we fall in love, we have to initially describe what took place. For our own awareness of the wonder unfolding in such love, we have to name the wonder aloud.

But love isn't just a single event. As we grow mature in love, we want couples to more clearly articulate the wisdom that has come from being in love with this person. So too, we must move the neophytes from the powerful experience to a reasonable articulation of what took place in the rite. What is the wisdom revealed to the church through the blessing of a candle? Through the baptismal waters? Through the Eucharist? How can this wisdom transform my own life?

In addition to reflecting on the Vigil, the period of mystagogy is the right time to teach a way of reading time in a liturgical key. What do I mean? During the season of Easter, we come to see how every dimension of human life can be transformed through the resurrection. On Easter, food is blessed. Water is blessed. All creation is blessed. Thus, we're especially aware at this time of the way that the church can bless all of life, all of time, all of space. Everything.

It's appropriate during Easter mystagogy to once again return to the practice of the Liturgy of the Hours. Those who were baptized at Easter could receive the four-volume set of the Liturgy of the Hours. They could be taught, perhaps by a group within the parish, to pray the Hours, and the Easter Season is an especially great occasion to give a basic catechesis to the whole parish on the transformative quality of the Hours.

The catechesis for the Hours should emphasize three dimensions. First, the Liturgy of the Hours is the prayer of Christ and the church that sanctifies all believers. To commit oneself to praying some of the Liturgy of the Hours is to exercise the priesthood of the entire Body of Christ, "to offer the worship of the New Covenant, a worship that derives not from our own powers but from Christ's merit and gift" (General Instruction on the Liturgy of the Hours, 7). Praying the Hours is therefore the appropriate act of those who have been baptized into this holy priesthood. Our speech has been taken up, transfigured, through our relationship with Jesus Christ. We now speak not just for ourselves but also for the whole church when we pray the Hours in community. We speak as Christ when we pray with all believers.

Second, the Liturgy of the Hours consecrates each hour of the day. We rise to praise God in the morning, recognizing that the rising sun is a sign of Christ. We interrupt our noonday meal to consider Christ's death on a cross. At the end of the day, we consecrate the setting sun and our sleep to Christ, aware of all the ways that we have also sinned. For the one who prays the Hours, the mystery of Christ pervades every hour of every day. The whole day becomes oriented toward God.

Third, the Liturgy of the Hours also steeps the memory of Christians with those salutary images of salvation that suffuse the whole Christian year. The Office of Readings introduces one into the history of contemplating the mystery of Christ. We pray with Catherine of Siena and Augustine of Hippo, with the documents from Vatican II and accounts of martyrs. Likewise, the Scriptures themselves come to be written on our memory. The *Benedictus* and the *Magnificat* become our songs.

Finally, the parish can promote this mystagogy through devoting Easter in particular to liturgical formation. Families can be taught the Liturgy of the Hours. We might hold icon-writing seminars in the parish, with some of the icons being used in the eucharistic liturgy of the parish. We should hold processions with the Eucharist. We should set aside special time to celebrate First Communions, marriages, ordinations to the priesthood, and other parish feasts. The bulletin could be filled with articles from parishioners describing the fruits of the sacramental life—telling about the way that life in Christ, lived most fully in the Eucharist, has transformed them. Just as Lent was an occasion of penance, Easter should be six weeks of feasting.

Pentecost is the culminating moment of the mystagogical period. For on this feast, the church celebrates the descent of the Spirit in the upper room in Jerusalem. The feast of Pentecost is the birthday of the church as a liturgical and sacramental body. A mystagogical parish will celebrate this feast with the festivity it deserves, including the special vigil with the extended readings. The accounts of the conquering of the Tower of Babel in Genesis, the giving of the law on Mount Sinai in Exodus, the raising of the dry bones in Ezekiel, and the promise of the gift of the spirit in the prophet Joel provide an *inclusio* with the Easter Vigil. Just as Christ's resurrection was promised, so too is the descent of the Spirit. Paul's description of the Spirit as aiding us in our weakness and the Gospel of John's promise of the Spirit completes the cycle of readings at the Vigil.

Pentecost and its vigil are a fitting end to Easter for the neophytes. They have been incorporated into Christ's Body through the sacraments, and now they begin their mission to the ends of the world. The collect prayer for the Vigil Mass asks:

> Almighty ever-living God,
> who willed the Paschal Mystery
> to be encompassed as a sign in fifty days,
> grant that from out of the scattered nations
> the confusion of many tongues
> may be gathered by heavenly grace
> into one great confession of your name.
>
> (*Roman Missal*, Pentecost, At the Vigil Mass)

The erstwhile catechumens have been incorporated into the church, the body that transcends language, race, and class. And now they have a vocation to assist the church in gathering all humanity into the church. The divine blessing they have received from God is now the grace that they are to offer to their brothers and sisters.

The Mystagogy of Parish Life

One of the problems with Easter mystagogy is its brevity. That is, a parish that does this kind of mystagogy for a couple of weeks during the Easter Season might not be able to sustain a mystagogical habit throughout the rest of the liturgical year. In this parish, the habit will likely not be sustained beyond the Easter Season.

Mystagogy, though, can be celebrated throughout the year. Many parishes, for example, have taken up the habit of doing small-group Scripture studies for evangelization. In these studies, they read the Scriptures and share how they see the Good News in their own lives. This is a type of theological reflection in which the Scriptures shape how we tell our own stories. The Gospel is incarnated within our lives.

Too often, liturgical texts are not part of these Bible studies. Yet it is precisely the liturgical texts that show us how the mystery of Christ is unfolding here and now. These texts help us read the Scriptures, better pray the liturgy, and see God's activity in our life.

Let's imagine that a parish has decided to do a liturgically oriented study of the Scriptures. On the Twelfth Sunday in Ordinary Time, the *Missal* includes texts for an entrance antiphon taken from Psalm 28, an opening prayer, a prayer over the offerings, two possible communion antiphons, and a prayer after Communion. The prayer over the offerings expresses a common theme found in nearly every Mass:

> Receive, O Lord, the sacrifice of conciliation and praise
> and grant that, cleansed by its action,
> we may make offering of a heart pleasing to you.
> Through Christ our Lord. (*Roman Missal*)

This prayer will initially be a bit confusing. Most likely, few will understand what conciliation means! Conciliation means a sacrificial offering that brings two different groups together. It's a mediating, peace offering. Therefore, the prayer asks that, through making this offering of peace, of praise, the entire assembly may be cleansed of its sin, capable of offering our whole hearts to God.

Here, this prayer gives ample space to talk not just about liturgy but also about life. Are there not places in our lives where we are in need of such a peace offering? Do we gossip about fellow colleagues, forestalling the friendship that the human family is called to enjoy? Do we enact violence on Twitter, creating a space where hatred rather than love reigns? In the Eucharist, we seek to give all of this over to God. We are cleansed, healed of this sin. And we become even more capable of offering our hearts to God. In the context of our small groups, we can hold ourselves accountable week-to-week to making our whole heart an offering to God.

Even a normal Sunday, such as the Twelfth Sunday in Ordinary Time, provides an occasion for mystagogy. The priest is not the only one responsible for offering these prayers with fullness of heart and mind. The whole parish is involved, and the more that each person has reflected on the meaning of the texts in their lives, the more likely they'll be able to pray the liturgy. The texts provide the foundation of a liturgical spirituality that is the cornerstone of the parish's mystagogy.

Texts are not the only dimension of mystagogy. One could imagine a parish series on the essential, embodied practices of the liturgy including standing, kneeling, singing, lighting candles, blessing ourselves with water, extending hands, and kissing icons. Each of these actions disposes us toward wisdom, toward a certain way of abiding in the world. When we kneel, we're not just engaging in a random practice. We're offering ourselves to God.

In the context of mystagogy, many parishes quote that famous phrase from St. Augustine's sermon 272: "Become what you receive, receive what you are." This "becoming" and "receiving" for St. Augustine is not reserved to the Eucharist. Each time we Christians worship, we "become" what we receive. When we light a candle, we are to become the light of the world. When we kneel before God, we are meant to become a creature who adores. When we bless ourselves with holy water, we are to become a temple of the Spirit. Continued instruction in the meaning of these postures can sustain a Christian through a lifetime.

Treating the liturgical texts and practice as a source of wisdom is essential to developing this mystagogical habit in the parish. If we are doing mystagogy during Advent and Christmas, during Lent and Easter, during Ordinary Time and on saints' feasts, we will discover that the whole parish "knows" how to do mystagogy. By the time the neophytes join the eucharistic assembly, they won't need a special six weeks to inculcate this mystagogical habit. It will be part of their whole life as Catholics, and they'll be able to participate with full mind, heart, and voice.

Conclusion

Mystagogy, for the neophyte, is an extension of the liturgical formation they have received throughout the catechumenate. In the Christian life, the beauty of the liturgy has provoked us. It has offered a hypothesis about the meaning of our lives, giving us a divine blessing that can sustain us from birth to death. It has been verified in our bodies, as we have been baptized, been confirmed, and received the Holy Eucharist. And now, the rest of our lives, we are called to reflect on what provokes us, what is proposed to us, and how we can become what we have received in the liturgy.

The irony of mystagogical catechesis is that it is best accomplished through a parish that cares about the liturgy—a parish that attends to the beauty of the signs of worship, a parish that sees its worship as taking up every dimension of human life in Christ, a parish that practices in love what it preaches. When we have become these kind of parishes, not only will mystagogy flourish, but we'll also find ourselves welcoming more catechumens seeking to adore the living God.

Bibliography

Benedict XVI, Pope. Message of His Eminence Cardinal Joseph Ratzinger to the Communion and Liberation Meeting at Rimini. August 24–30, 2002.

Catechism of the Catholic Church. 2nd ed. United States Catholic Conference— Libreria Editrice Vaticana, 1997.

Congregation for the Clergy. *General Directory for Catechesis.* Washington, DC: United States Catholic Conference, 1998.

Francis, Pope. *Laudato Si'.* Encyclical Letter on Care for Our Common Home. May 24, 2015.

———. Rejoice and Be Glad (*Gaudete et Exsultate*). Apostolic Exhortation on the Call to Holiness in Today's World. March 19, 2018.

———. The Joy of the Gospel (*Evangelii Gaudium*). Apostolic Exhortation on the Proclamation of the Gospel in Today's World. November 24, 2013.

Giussani, Luigi. *The Religious Sense.* Translated by John Zucchi. Ithaca, NY: McGill-Queen's University Press, 1997.

———. *The Risk of Education: Discovering Our Ultimate Destiny.* Translated by Rosanna M. Giammanco Frogia. New York: Crossroad, 2001.

———. *Why the Church?* Translated by Viviane Hewitt. Ithaca, NY: McGill-Queen's University Press, 2001.

Giussani, Luigi, Stefano Alberto, and Javier Prades. *Generating Traces in the History of the World: New Traces of the Christian Experience.* Translated by Patrick Stevenson. Ithaca, NY: McGill-Queen's University Press, 2010.

Rite of Christian Initiation of Adults. Study ed. Collegeville, MN: Liturgical Press, 1988.

Savorana, Alberto. *The Life of Luigi Giussani.* Translated by Mariangela C. Sullivan and Christopher Bacich. Montreal: McGill-Queen's University Press, 2018.

Vatican II Council. Constitution on the Sacred Liturgy (*Sacrosanctum Concilium*). December 4, 1963. In Austin Flannery, ed., *Vatican Council II: The Conciliar and Postconciliar Documents.* Collegeville, MN: Liturgical Press, 2014.

von Hildebrand, Dietrich. *Liturgy and Personality.* Steubenville, OH: Hildebrand Project, 2016.

CPSIA information can be obtained
at www.ICGtesting.com
Printed in the USA
LVHW020412170423
744530LV00021BA/300